Faith AT Work

MOSAICA PRESS

Faith AT Work

ELEVATING OUR WORK DAY
PARASHAH BY PARASHAH

INCLUDING INSPIRING
STORIES FROM THE OFFICE

JEFF WEINBERG

Published by Mosaica Press, Inc.
www.mosaicapress.com
info@mosaicapress.com

This *sefer* is dedicated to my beloved father

Mr. David Weinberg
DOVID BEN YOSEF, ZT"L

From the ashes of the Holocaust, my father, with strength
and *emunah*, found a way to ignite dying embers and
build a beautiful family that continues to carry the
torches of those that he lost. My father was a dedicated
and hardworking man, who provided for our family from
morning until night. While he labored in a foreign world
to bring us safety and security, his heart and soul were
occupied with the service of Hashem and in perpetuating
the Torah values of yesteryear. It is from him that
I learned what it means to live **in** this world but live **for**
another world, to do what needs to be done but be ever
aware and cognizant of what our life goals are. If you read
through this *sefer* and are perhaps inspired to live a more
elevated life, may it be *l'ilui nishmas* my dear father.

One of the inspirations for this *sefer* was
my dear father-in-law, our cherished Poppy.

Rabbi Dr. Fred Gross

PINCHAS BEN NOSSON CHANOCH, ZT"L

Our Poppy was a true inspiration. He fused his work with
his *avodas Hashem* in a remarkable way. As a world-class
mathematician, he remained a *ben Torah* in a secular
environment without really having a support system.
But the lessons we learned from him went far beyond
that. His love and awe of Hashem's beautiful world were
very pronounced—in his work and his life He taught
us by example that the study of Hashem's world, while
referred to as secular, can indeed be a source of great
spirituality and inspiration. When he studied and taught
mathematics, he felt that he was sharing the spiritual
experience of the wonder of Hashem's creation. We
found the following in his notes regarding the study of
science: "Scientific study is a source of deep spirituality,
a source of wonder, awe, beauty, symmetry...[a source
of] inspiration is the amazing simplicity of complex
structures...." As Poppy developed in his field, he also
was developing as a Jew. As he grew and advanced in
his profession, winning awards for his research, he was
ever-growing in his appreciation and love of Hashem.
May this *sefer*'s message, which he lived, be a *zechus*
for his amazing *neshamah*.

RABBI EFREM GOLDBERG   הרב אפרים חיים גולדברג
BOCA RATON SYNAGOGUE   ק״ק בית כנסת בוקא ראטון

HAHN JUDAIC CAMPUS · 7900 MONTOYA CIRCLE · BOCA RATON FL 33433
TEL 561.394.0394 · FAX 561.702.4198 · REG@BRSONLINE.ORG

בס״ד

April 26, 2021
14 Iyar 5781

To Whom It May Concern:

My dear friend Jeff Weinberg, in collaboration with
Rabbi Yisroel Simcha Weingot, share their inspiration
with us in a magnificent series of Divrei Torah that
not only elucidate the Parsha but make it relevant to
our daily lives.

Jeff and R' Weingot bring their wisdom and real-life
experiences to provide insights that not only inform
but inspire us towards more mindful and meaningful
living. I highly recommend not only adding their
Sefer to your library but sharing their Divrei Torah at
your Shabbos table.

Most sincerely,

Rabbi Efrem Goldberg

Rabbi Mordechai Kamenetzky
Rosh Yeshiva

April 15, 2021
3 Iyar 5781

To my dear friend and supporter of Torah and chessed world over, Jeff Weinberg, נ"י,

I am proud to write a few words as an approbation for your forthcoming book which I have perused with much excitement and enjoyment.

Over the past number of years, there have been a large array of wonderful *seforim* and books written by Rabbis and Roshei Yeshiva, that have focused on giving guidance and *chizuk* to Jewish people in the workforce.

Each one of them is important and adds to the greater library of Jewish inspirational literature that has become part and parcel of Jewish life in America.

In his wonderful work "Faith at Work" Chaim Yosef Yaakov Weinberg, or as he is called in the world of business … Jeff, has done something even more special. Jeff is not a rabbi, and he is not a Rosh Yeshiva. He is a businessperson. His *sefer* brings wonderful Torah perspectives to the world of business, through the eyes of a businessman.

Spiced with beautiful stories from *tzadikim* throughout history, and anecdotes from his vast personal experiences, Jeff brings a refreshing relatable approach that is easily palatable to anyone who has ever sat behind an office desk, or worked in the field while trying to support his family. He intersperses *Divrei Torah* on each *parsha* with his business acumen and personal involvement to meld the world of ואספת דגנך --making a living, with the world of ודברת בם -- learning Torah and leading a Torah life.

The book is filled with life lessons in *emunah* and *hashgacha*, faith and Divine providence that can be applied every day in every situation.

Our *Chazal* in *Mesechtas Shabbos* tell us that after 120 years, when we come to Heaven, one of the questions we will be asked by the *Beis Din Shel Maalah*, the Heavenly Tribunal is, "נָשָׂאתָ וְנָתַתָּ בָּאֱמוּנָה? Did you conduct your business faithfully?" Others comment that this is not only a question about honesty, but about having faith in the workplace as well.

Reading this *sefer* is definitely a way to help one be able to answer the question in the affirmative.

May *Hashem* Bless you and your entire family with much *nachas* and *gezunt* and continue to bestow His blessings upon you for continued success in your *parnasah* which has been a true model of "Faith at Work."

With Torah blessings,

Mordechai Kamenetzky

Rabbi Yehoshua Kurland

It is a great privilege for me to extend my *divrei berachah* to my dear and beloved friend R' Jeff Weinberg in regard to his beautiful *sefer* on *parashas hashavua* that has such a unique flavor and quality. I have long advocated to others who are working, to never relinquish their dream to write a *sefer*, thinking that they either lack the ability or erudition to do so. The power of *chiddush* is something embedded deep in the Jewish soul that surfaces when tapped into and of course met with tremendous *siyata d'Shmaya*. If there is anyone who is capable of producing a *sefer* that maximizes the brilliance of novel thought in Torah with life experiences as a successful businessman it is Jeff. He is a true *oveid Hashem* whose primary focus is *deveikus* in the RBSO and in His Torah as he somehow manages to conduct business as a partner in a very prestigious company. His approach toward life is one fully guided by his steadfast *emunah* that it is Hashem who runs the world and we humble ourselves to His *ratzon*.

I sincerely believe that this volume will serve as a great source of *chizuk* to those attempting to acclimate and transition from the *beis medrash* to the working world and prove that the dictum of Chazal of *ein beis medrash b'lo chiddush* applies everywhere when one takes the *beis medrash* with him as R' Jeff does.

May Hashem shower him and his wonderful *mishpachah* with a *shefa* of *berachah v'hatzlachah* in the *zechus* of this monumental work and all of his philanthropy for *Klal Yisroel*.

בידידות ובאהבת לב ונפש
יהושע קורלאנד

Congregation Aish Kodesh
of Woodmere
351 Midwood Road
Woodmere, N. Y. 11598
516 - 569-2660

RABBI MOSHE WEINBERGER

ב"ה

ח' אייר תשפ"א

The remarkable sefer that you are holding in your hands reflects years of dedicated learning of two of the most beloved and extraordinary people in my life. My dear son in law, Rabbi Yisroel Simcha Weingot א"שליט, and my friend and soulmate Jeff Weinberg have been chavrusos for many, many years. Over the course of time they have been painstakingly making their way through Shas, blatt by blatt, perek by perek, Masechta by Masechta. R. Weingot, a seasoned Talmid Chacham and Maggid shiur, and Jeff, a successful professional and lover of Torah, are holy thieves who literally steal every available minute of their busy lives to grab another Rashi and Tosafos, another Rambam and Ra'avad.

"Faith At Work" is not the result of any pre-meditated plan to make a new contribution to the growing corpus of English Torah literature. It is a journal of Jeff's determination to equip himself with the depth and beauty of Torah in order to rise above the materialism and permissiveness that pervade the modern-day workplace. Over the years Jeff has reflected and expounded upon many drashos, shiurim, and divrei Torah that served as his life-line to kedushah, emunah, and bitachon. The Torah was not meant to be confined to the Beis Medrash. It is the key to an elevated existence in the home, the office, as well as the motel room on a lonely business trip stopover.

I urge you to study and be inspired by this wonderful sefer.

TABLE OF CONTENTS

Sefer Shemos

Sefer Bamidbar

Sefer Devarim

PREFACE

"What are you writing, Dad?" my son asked me when he was nine years old.

"I am trying to write a *sefer*," I told him. "But Dad, you are not a rabbi!" He was right. I am not a rabbi, a writer, or a scholar for that matter. I am simply a *shomer Shabbos* Jew who has been going to work to earn a *parnassah* for my family for the past thirty-five years. "So, what are you writing about?" he continued.

That is what I would like to share with you.

Having been in the workplace for all these years, I have felt a strong pull to write about the role and attitude of the *shomer Shabbos* Jew who is going to work every day to provide for his family. I felt a need to discuss and expand on how the Torah views the working Jew, and how we can learn the lessons through the eyes of each *parashah* on what our hashkafic attitude should be as we head out to the office.

For those of us who have been working for a long time, and for those who are starting out in their careers, there is an important message I would like to share. Many think that once we leave the shul or *beis midrash* in the morning, our connection with Hashem is interrupted or put on hold until we get back home or until we daven *Minchah*. Nothing could be further from the truth! We have an amazing *achrayus* and *zechus* to be able to serve Hashem all day long—whether at our desks, behind our computers, on the phone, or face-to-face with our customers or clients. What I have tried to do in this *sefer* is to bring this feeling into reality with the timeless messages from our weekly *sidrah*, combined with personal stories from experiences from the working world—both mine and those of my clients and friends. I hope that you will find this *sefer* to be insightful, and may it bring more meaning and inspiration into your workday.

I would like to thank and acknowledge those who have helped me along this journey. First of all, my parents, Mr. David Weinberg (Dovid ben Yosef), *a"h*, and *l'havdil bein chaim l'chaim*, my mother, Mrs. Erna Weinberg, for giving me such a special home to grow up in and for teaching me and my sisters how to live as good and proud Jews. My father, a survivor of the Holocaust, worked very hard for many years in the motor-and-pump business to provide for us and to make sure to rebuild so much that was taken from him. I remember him washing his precious hands every day after work and the sink turning a dark black from all the machinery grease he was washing off.

To my *rav*, Rav Moshe Weinberger of Aish Kodesh in Woodmere, New York: Rebbi, what can I say? My wife and I were lucky enough to "stumble" into the Woodmere community over twenty-eight years ago, and little did we know what was waiting for our family there. Rebbi and Rebbetzin, thank you so much for all the *chizuk* and inspiration you have given us over the years. We feel truly blessed that we have the *zechus* to be part of your wonderful *kehillah* and family. May you continue to inspire us and so many around the world in good health with your lessons on how we are supposed to live our lives.

To my amazing *chavrusa*, R' Yisroel Simcha Weingot: R' Simchie, I am so grateful for the first time we bumped into each other. You and Suri have been such an inspiration to our family, and we are forever grateful. Your home is a source of *simchah* that we take as an example of how beautiful and real Yiddishkeit really is! Thank you both so much for helping my dream come true with this *sefer*. Needless to say, I definitely couldn't have done it without your help!

To Rabbi Yaacov Haber and Rabbi Doron Kornbluth and the entire wonderful staff at Mosaica Press, for all your help and guidance. And to my colleagues and friends who have helped sponsor this *sefer*, Ralph Herzka, Rael Gervis, Cary Pollack, Dovid Ostrov, and Moshe Majeski.

To our wonderful children with whom Hashem has blessed us: Tali and Adam, Tamara and Hesh, Yonina and Shlomo, Zehava and Shlomo #2, Dassi, Shana, and Shua. Mommy and I are so proud of who you have become and how you continue to grow in such a beautiful way. Thank you for helping me as you listened to a lot of the *divrei Torah* in this book and for your wonderful suggestions along the way. May you continue to give all of us and Hashem tremendous *nachas*!

And, *acharon acharon chaviv*, to my dear wife, Sharona: Thank you so much for all the support you have given and continue to give me. I don't know how you do it, taking care of our family and all the responsibilities that go with it when I am not around most of the time. It's one thing to do the job right, but another to do it with such love and care, and you are able to do it all! I am in awe of you!

And finally, I thank the Ribbono Shel Olam, the source of all blessing! Thank You for giving me this opportunity to hopefully make an impact on Your children as they take on a life of truly holy work.

Jeff Weinberg
Woodmere, New York
Adar 5781

Sefer Bereishis

Bereishis

THE GREATEST CATCH OF ALL

וַיְבָרֶךְ אֱלֹקִים אֶת יוֹם הַשְּׁבִיעִי וַיְקַדֵּשׁ
אֹתוֹ כִּי בוֹ שָׁבַת מִכָּל מְלַאכְתּוֹ אֲשֶׁר
בָּרָא אֱלֹקִים לַעֲשׂוֹת.

And God blessed the seventh day, and
sanctified it; because in it He rested from all
His work that God in creating had made.

Bereishis 2:3

We are taught that Shabbos is the source of all blessings. As we say in *Lechah Dodi* every Friday night: "כִּי הִיא מְקוֹר הַבְּרָכָה—For it [Shabbos] is the source of blessing."

Quite often, the Chafetz Chaim would respond to those who were seeking his blessings: "I am not the source of blessing; Shabbos is! Be careful to observe Shabbos, and you will receive blessing. Shabbos has no connection to the curse of Adam, 'By the sweat of your brow you will eat bread.' That is only referring to the six days of work. On the contrary, Shabbos infuses endless blessing throughout the whole week."

The *Zohar* teaches us that Shabbos is one of the names of Hashem. The source of all good comes from Hashem. Just as we refrain from work on Shabbos, and we clearly see the blessing from Hashem, so too, the more we realize that it is all truly from Hashem, the more the blessing

3

will flow! This realization should encourage us to usher in Shabbos as soon as we can and to hold onto it for as long as we are able.

This can be clarified with the following analogy: When a large fish is chasing a smaller fish, wanting to eat it, as soon as the large fish catches up to him and is ready to eat it, another small fish makes his way toward him head on. This small fish becomes the meal instead. If the larger fish would have caught the original fish, he would not have had a meal but would have died, as the direction of the scales "were" open toward him. The scales of the smaller fish would have ripped at his throat, killing him. But the fish who swims in the opposite direction and has scales facing the opposite direction can smoothly enter the larger fish, not even causing a scratch.

All week, we chase our livelihood. We follow what we think will bring us "the next meal." We try to get a "great catch." However, what ultimately comes our way is a gift from Hashem, sometimes in the opposite direction of what we were initially pursuing.

About twenty years ago, I was trying to get Mr. Goldstein* as a client. I constantly attempted to contact him, but to no avail. After a few years, I stopped trying. Seventeen years later, I received a call from another client. He was at a meeting with someone who was trying to buy a building from him. Who was this "someone"? None other than Mr. Goldstein, whom I had tried reaching so many years back. My client suggested that he call me to get help with the deal. The rest is history! We got that deal and more since! I tried, I stopped, and Hashem delivered.

The *pasuk* ends with the word לַעֲשׂוֹת—to do. As much as we take heed of the lessons of Shabbos, namely that Hashem is the ultimate source of *berachah*, may we merit to see blessing with our לַעֲשׂוֹת, our work.

BRAINSTORMING

וּמֵעֵץ הַדַּעַת טוֹב וָרָע לֹא תֹאכַל
מִמֶּנּוּ כִּי בְּיוֹם אֲכָלְךָ מִמֶּנּוּ
מוֹת תָּמוּת.

But as for the tree of knowledge of good and
bad, you must not eat of it; for as soon as
you eat of it, you shall die.

Bereishis 2:17

The only restriction given to Adam was that he was forbidden to eat from the *Eitz Ha'daas.* Why was this the only prohibition? We know that the Torah and Chazal often refer to our *parnassah* as *"mezonos."* Perhaps we can suggest that the message here is this: As we are thrown back into our work after the *Yamim Noraim*, we must remember that we don't eat because of our *daas*—brilliance. Hashem is our sole provider. Sometimes, we get a brilliant idea or have just the right words to make the deal happen; we can feel ownership over that and credit our *daas* to the subsequent success that comes. We must remember that it is all from our Creator.

The term that is used in business when people join together to think of ideas is "brainstorming." The term itself is indicative of the fallacy that we often fall prey to. It gives us a false sense of pride in ourselves and our brainpower.

> *Once, an old priest put up his forest for sale. A chassid of Reb Dovid Moshe of Chortkov, zt"l, was very interested in buying it. He met with the priest to discuss the details, and then the Yid spoke to his financial advisors. Everyone agreed that this was "the deal of a lifetime." The price was extremely low, and he could sell the lumber and earn a nice profit. But before finalizing the deal, the chassid wanted a berachah from his Rebbe.*
>
> *Because the Yid did not doubt that he should buy the forest, he expected to just get the Rebbe's blessings. The Rebbe told him that he doesn't think he should buy the forest. The Yid was devastated; how could he turn down such a lucrative investment? In his eyes, it was like throwing away a fortune. He decided that he wouldn't listen to the Rebbe this time, and he went ahead and bought the forest.*
>
> *When he sent workers to cut some of the trees, the problem was discovered. The trees were rotting, wormy, and thus valueless. For the next two years, the Yid was embarrassed to visit his Rebbe, knowing that he foolishly lost so much money because he didn't listen to his Rebbe's wise counsel. But one day, he told himself, "It is bad enough that I lost money. Should I lose my Rebbe too?" and he traveled to Chortkov.*
>
> *Immediately upon meeting the Rebbe, he said, "I know, it is my fault. I didn't listen to the Rebbe's ruach hakodesh…"*
>
> *The Rebbe corrected him, "My counsel didn't come from ruach hakodesh. It was logical. I saw that you were so certain that you would earn a lot of money from this investment, and this attitude frightened me because you forgot that it is impossible to succeed without Hashem's help. When you consulted me, you didn't say, 'b'ezras Hashem,' not even once. Therefore, I told you that you shouldn't invest in the forest, because an investment without Hashem is doomed to failure."*

As we "storm" out of the most beautiful time of the year, i.e., the *Yamim Nora'im*, and head back to work, let's remember that our *daas* isn't what brings the *mezonos*—the *parnassah*. If we remember this, we will, *im yirtzeh Hashem*, find success in many areas of our lives.

Noach

THE LOFTY PROVIDER

נֹחַ אִישׁ צַדִּיק.

Noach was a righteous man.
Bereishis 6:9

How did Noach merit such a prestigious title?

The Midrash provides us with an amazing idea and a powerful lesson. Noach is called a *tzaddik* because he provided for others. He took care of all those animals that were with him in the ark.

One may think that such a title should be given to one who spends every moment toiling in the "Sea of Torah," the holiest of tasks. However, the Midrash teaches us who truly deserves the title—someone who feeds others. And not only people, but even animals!

We find another person that received this title as well: Yosef. Why did he earn it? Was it because of the superhuman strength that Yosef displayed with the wife of Potiphar? No. He received the name because he was a provider, as Yosef told his brothers: "כִּי לְמִחְיָה שְׁלָחַנִי—For I was sent to be a provider.[1]"

Two great people who both did many great things, and yet what earned them the title of *tzaddik* was their shared *middah* of giving.

---

1   *Bereishis* 45:5.

8

I know someone who grew up in a home where the *middah* of giving was an evident priority. While the cleaning help would alleviate some of the day-to-day stress involved in running a home, she was never allowed to change the linens in the guest room. This act of *hachnasas orchim* was reserved for the children. Their mother would say that there are certain acts of giving, such as welcoming guests, that she doesn't want anyone but her kids to reap the benefit and rewards of. It is too priceless an opportunity to give away.

There are times when you may feel that because you were busy in the office all day, you didn't properly serve Hashem—that your learning a bit in the morning and grabbing a *shiur* at night is all you did. Just remember, however, as you work to provide for your family—for the children of Hashem—whom you are emulating. Remember as you give tzedakah to your extended family and to those in your circles that you are emulating the ways of these two *tzaddikim*. As you focus on why you are working, you will not toil with "busy" work, but rather with holy work.

May we all merit the title of *tzaddik*, as Rav Moshe Meir Weiss says, "Who is a *tzaddik*? One who is פּוֹתֵחַ אֶת יָדֶךָ—who opens their hand. Isn't it amazing that the word that follows this *pasuk* in *Ashrei* is…*tzaddik*?!"

Lech Lecha

THE ROAD NOT TAKEN

וַיִּקְחוּ אֶת לוֹט וְאֶת רְכֻשׁוֹ
בֶּן אֲחִי אַבְרָם וַיֵּלֵכוּ.

And they took Lot, and his possessions,
the nephew of Avraham, and they went.
Bereishis 14:12

his *pasuk* seems to be out of order. It should have said, "They took Lot, who is Avraham's nephew, and all of his possessions." Why is it written this way—the possessions before Lot's lineage?

Rabbi Yissachar Frand quotes Rav Shimon Schwab, who said as follows: At first, Lot seemed to be doing just fine spiritually. His travel partner was none other than Avraham Avinu. The Torah says that Lot, "הַהֹלֵךְ אֶת אַבְרָם—Went with Avram,"[1] i.e., as an equal. Furthermore, Avraham says about them, "For we are brothers."[2] They seemed to be on the same path. Yet, we know that Lot left all of his spiritual glory and chose to travel to Sodom, the capital of all evil. What happened?

Lot began to shift directions when he lost sight of the purpose of his wealth. He became "לוֹט וְאֶת רְכֻשׁוֹ—Lot and his possessions." He fell

---

1   *Bereishis* 13:5.
2   Ibid. v. 8.

into a life of materialism until it defined who he was. Now we can understand the order of the *pasuk*. First, it says his name, "לוֹט וְאֶת רְכֻשׁוֹ," because that was what his name was attached to, and then it tells us that he was the nephew of Avraham.

We all have the Avraham Avinu in our life that we can connect to. That is our *ruchniyus* and service of God. It is our davening, our family, and our *middos*; it is ultimately every moment of opportunity to fulfill *ratzon Hashem*. Yet, we have the constant *nisayon* of "the good life," i.e., the רְכוּשׁ, the possessions. They too have a purpose. It's our purpose to recognize their purpose.

> *As Rosh Yeshiva in Baranovitch, Rav Elchanan Wasserman frequently found it necessary to go elsewhere to raise funds for the yeshiva's upkeep. After many efforts in Europe with little success, he decided to travel to the United States.*
>
> *There, he was referred to a wealthy Jew named Philip Goldstein with whom Rav Wasserman had learned together in cheder as a boy. Mr. Goldstein was now the wealthy owner of a coat factory, but had long since abandoned Judaism and rarely donated to Torah institutions.*
>
> *A meeting was arranged, and the two met and shared memories of their childhood, and spoke about what each had been doing since then. After being brought up to date, Rav Wasserman turned to leave. Mr. Goldstein was confused.*
>
> *"But…didn't you come here for something?" he asked, alluding to the fact that Rav Wasserman had surely intended to ask for a donation to his yeshiva.*
>
> *"As a matter of fact, I did come for something. I have a problem. There are loose buttons on my coat, and I know that you have a coat factory. Could one of your employees come and tighten up the buttons?" asked Rav Elchanan, pointing to the loose button.*
>
> *Confused, Mr. Goldstein summoned an employee by telephone to come to repair Rav Wasserman's coat. The employee tightened all the buttons.*

"Now come on," said Mr. Goldstein. "You must have come here for something more important than fixing loose buttons."

"No, that really was my reason," said Rav Wasserman, as he thanked his friend once again and left.

The following day, Mr. Goldstein called Rav Wasserman and asked that he come to him again. Rav Wasserman arrived and found Mr. Goldstein in an agitated state.

"It just doesn't make sense. No one travels all the way from Europe to America just to fix loose buttons. You could have had this done for yourself right there in Baranovitch. Why did you come to me?"

"I already told you. I really came to you just for the buttons," replied Rav Wasserman.

"That's ridiculous! Tell the truth; didn't you come to ask for a donation to your yeshiva?"

"Let me explain what I meant," began Rav Wasserman. "You refuse to accept that I would come such a long way just to tighten a few buttons. So, I ask you: Why do you think that Hashem sent you from the Heavens above all the way down to this world? Just to sew a few buttons? This is the reason why you're here? All I did was travel a few thousand miles, whereas you came all the way from under Hashem's throne of glory, and for what? To sew a few buttons?"

Mr. Goldstein got the message. That same day he began keeping mitzvos again. He also began giving generously to Torah institutions, and helped the Baranovitch Yeshiva for many years.

May we all merit to utilize our possessions for the intent they were created, and realize that the ultimate purpose of all we have is to serve Hashem.

Vayeira

THE LOGIC OF THE ILLOGICAL

עַתָּה יָדַעְתִּי כִּי יְרֵא אֱלֹקִים אַתָּה.

Now I know that you are God-fearing.
Bereishis 22:12

As Avraham Avinu passes his tests with flying colors, he reaches the climax of it all with the test of *Akeidas Yitzchak*. After this amazing feat, which we benefit from until today, Hashem tells Avraham that he now sees what a God-fearing man Avraham truly is. Was Hashem not able to see that until now? The first nine tests were also difficult and demanded tremendous inner strength. Why does Hashem say, "**Now** I realize that you are a God-fearing person"? What was specifically unique about this that he only earned this title now?

This specific test seemed to go completely against what Hashem had promised Avraham earlier. Avraham had been told that his family would grow through Yitzchak, and now he was being told to kill him and the future generations along with him. Then, just as he was about to follow through with what he was told to do, Avraham was told not to lift a hand to slaughter him. It is after these seemingly contradictory statements and events that Hashem told him, "Now I know that you are God-fearing." Until then, he followed Hashem through nine tests with logic and *emunah*. With this ultimate test, he proved that he was able to

13

follow through on the commandments of Hashem, even when his logic would dictate the complete opposite.

The entire world, including our brain and our ability to think logical and coherent thoughts, is a direct creation of the Will of Hashem. Can I truly think that my logic is greater than the One who created logic? To question the logic of Hashem isn't logical! A *yarei Shamayim* is one who sees that what truly makes sense is following *ratzon Hashem*.

> In the early 1900s, a struggling Jew named Mr. Cohen* had difficulty making a parnassah when he found himself fired each weekend for keeping Shabbos. He eventually decided to open his own business selling window treatments. He struggled to make ends meet, but he was happy because he chose to celebrate Shabbos and become his own boss. Every Friday, he made sure to close a few hours before Shabbos so that he could properly prepare.
>
> One Erev Shabbos, a hotel manager entered his shop, looking to purchase window treatments. After looking through the different samples, he was getting close to placing an order. As the hour was late, Mr. Cohen informed him that he had to close his shop, but would be happy to continue on Sunday. The businessman was annoyed and couldn't understand why the shopkeeper couldn't stay open for a few more hours until the order was completed. The shopkeeper explained that he had accepted upon himself, for the sake of his religion, to close his shop with enough time to properly prepare for the holy Sabbath, and that even if he needed the business, he would understand if the businessman would seek his window shades elsewhere. The businessman left, quite unhappy.
>
> Sunday morning, as Mr. Cohen came to open up his store, he saw the hotel manager waiting for him. He said that he was upset at first, but then realized how impressive Mr. Cohen's actions really were. He then placed a large order.

Shortly after this incident, business began picking up tremendously for Mr. Cohen. Order after order came in, and word spread about the wonderful window treatments that were made in Mr. Cohen's shop. Years later, Mr. Cohen met that original hotel manager and expressed his appreciation for giving him that business in his early years, and he told him about how his business had picked up shortly after that incident. The hotel manager told him that he had been at a conference with other hotel owners a short while after he purchased Mr. Cohen's window treatments, and there he had let all the hotel owners know about Mr. Cohen's shop and about his religious devotion. He guaranteed the hotel owners that since Mr. Cohen was willing to lose money for his religious beliefs, his honesty and integrity will make doing business with him an absolute pleasure. Sure enough, they followed through on his recommendation.

This Yid made a decision to possibly lose out for the sake of Shabbos, and ultimately it was that seemingly illogical decision that may have "opened up windows" for opportunity.

May we merit to know that the greatest book of logic is the Torah, and while the ways of Hashem may not always make sense to us, it is through following Him, regardless, that will ultimately make "cents"!

Chayei Sarah

YIDDISHE GELT

וְלָקַחְתָּ אִשָּׁה לִבְנִי לְיִצְחָק.

And you shall take a wife for my son,
for Yitzchak.

Bereishis 24:4

Avraham Avinu was preparing his loyal servant, Eliezer, to seek a wife for his son, Yitzchak. *Rashi* explains that he wrote a contract that stated that he handed his wealth over to his son, which would convince his relatives that Yitzchak is financially capable of supporting a family.

This should make us stop and question what seems to be a shocking "deed." Avraham Avinu was the *Gadol Hador*, the greatest *kiruv* personality of all time! Can't he bank on that? Wouldn't that be enough of an honor for any future family? Their daughter would be entering the most prestigious family of the generation!

Here is where we learn about the power and the gift of materialism. It has a strong purpose—when used properly. If we use it to bring out its true *tachlis*, the sparks of holiness find a home. If used to help another Jew or to give *menuchas ha'nefesh* to family members, then it is serving its purpose. In fact, each dollar bill in our possession reminds us, "In God We Trust."

I know a special Jew who truly lives with this mindset every waking moment. His family once went on vacation to Disneyworld. After a fun-filled day, they left the park and headed back to the hotel. At some point, this Yid realized that it was almost time for *Minchah*, and the only minyan in the area was back in the park. The park would not let him back in unless he paid for a ticket, which was quite a hefty sum. Without hesitating, he purchased the ticket, enjoyed *Minchah* with a minyan, and then rejoined his family. That was holy money! It wasn't paper dollar bills; it was the key that allowed him to daven with a minyan.

A Yid en route to Eretz Yisrael was looking forward to enjoying the comforts of traveling business class. As he checked in at JFK, he was told that due to the extra luggage he had, he would be charged an additional one hundred dollars. A pretty insignificant amount, compared to the price of a business class ticket. However, a bystander, who was blessed with financial comfort, overheard and said, "I have only one bag, and yet I am entitled to two." When the first man hesitated to bother him, he said, "*Chaval* on *Yiddishe gelt!*"

Rav Meir of Premishlan once announced on Rosh Hashanah: "Ribbono Shel Olam! I know if You will squeeze out the *tefillos* and supplications with which the Yidden turn to You all year, You will find *tefillos* about money. *Parnassah* is no small matter. And so, we turn to You and daven for *parnassah*.

"On the other hand, if You will squeeze out our money, You will find many mitzvos. Because what does a Yid need money for if not to do mitzvos? A Yid wants to marry off his daughter to a *talmid chacham*, pay for a *melamed* to learn with the children, buy an esrog, etc."

The Premishlaner concluded with a rousing *tefillah*. "Hakadosh Baruch Hu, we beg You, please send us *parnassah* so that we can serve You better!"

May we merit an understanding of the holiness of "*Yiddishe gelt!*" Whether it is buying us a *Minchah*, buying lunch for a hungry Yid, or providing for our family, it is holy money.

A MATTER OF WHAT MATTERS

וְאַשְׁבִּיעֲךָ בַּה׳ אֱלֹקֵי הַשָּׁמַיִם וֵאלֹקֵי
הָאָרֶץ אֲשֶׁר לֹא תִקַּח אִשָּׁה לִבְנִי
מִבְּנוֹת הַכְּנַעֲנִי אֲשֶׁר אָנֹכִי יוֹשֵׁב
בְּקִרְבּוֹ.

And I will make you swear by the God of
the Heavens and the God of the Earth, that
you will not take a wife for my son from the
daughters of Canaan that dwell in his midst.

Bereishis 24:3

Why would Avraham have Eliezer swear before he set out on his mission to find a wife for Yitzchak? We know that taking an oath is a big deal, as swearing in vain is one of the *Aseres Hadibros*. The Torah writes, concerning those who swear in vain, "God will not forgive"! Furthermore, the Gemara says that even those who are suspected of thievery and can't be trusted with money can be trusted with a *shevuah*. Such is the Torah power of an oath. What was of such importance here that a *shevuah* was necessary? Was Avraham trying to protect his wealth? Was the *shevuah* protecting him in the event that Eliezer would be financially negligent?

No. Rather, the *shevuah* was for the purpose of making sure that Eliezer finds a *kallah* suitable for Yitzchak—someone with Torah ideals and values.

We can tell what is important to a person by the time, energy, and investment that they give to that particular matter. Where do they take the most caution? The areas of our life that we plan and schedule, check, and recheck are the areas we consider most important.

My friend's wife always says to him, "It is the things in life that get you worked up that show what you are truly *machshiv*." Does it bother us when we come two minutes late to a *Shacharis*? Or when we come two minutes late to a baseball game? Would we dare come late to the office meeting as the CEO? Yet, for *Shacharis*…that we can quickly catch up. How many spreadsheets and calculations are made to measure the growth of the business? Have we ever made a *cheshbon ha'nefesh*, an inner calculation of what truly matters—how we treat our wives? Our children? Are we faithful to our employer, our spouse and ultimately, the Creator? Before planning a trip, what are the crucial considerations? The view from the hotel window or the minyan? The dessert menu or the kashrus? The big-name entertainers or the purity of our eyes?

Before Eliezer set out, there was one matter that Avraham Avinu made sure was taken care of—that his son should have a pure wife. The rest was entrusted to Eliezer, who the Torah described as "הַמּשֵׁל בְּכָל אֲשֶׁר לוֹ—The one who controlled all that was his."[1] But in one area—the future of his son's *ruchniyus*—Avraham went so far as to make Eliezer take a *shevuah*.

A good friend of mine, who is a long-time real-estate syndicator/developer, works extremely hard and puts in long hours each day. However, he is very strict to set aside time to learn every day, and he made a decision that the most important *seder* he was going to keep was having dinner with his family every night at 6:30. No matter which big deal is pending or how much work he has to do, he shuts off his phone and is there for family time each and every night. When I mentioned

---

1   *Bereishis* 24:2.

this to the CEO of a very successful company, he jokingly told me he will immediately institute the same practice one night a week, and he chose Friday night!

When I speak and meet many young men who are starting out in the workforce today, there seems to be a tremendous demand on them to work very long hours and sometimes even weekends when they start out. We obviously cannot judge or make decisions for these young men, as every situation must be analyzed individually, but maybe we can suggest that they really look at all the options available and make a decision that will be best for their *ruchniyus* and *gashmiyus*.

May we merit a life of priority—days that are spent in *chesbon ha'nefesh* of our spiritual stocks and inventory.

KEEP IT FRESH

אוּלַי לֹא תֹאבֶה הָאִשָּׁה לָלֶכֶת אַחֲרָי.

Maybe the woman will not wish
to follow me.

Bereishis 24:5

Eliezer said this statement to Avraham in regard to finding a wife for Yitzchak. We see that there is a *vav* in the word, אוּלַי—maybe. This *vav* was not written when Eliezer is later speaking to Besuel. There, the word אוּלַי is spelled without the *vav*—אֻלַי.[1]

Rashi tells us that when Eliezer said this statement to Avraham, he had a hope that Yitzchak would marry his own daughter and that Rivkah would not follow him back to Yitzchak. He had hoped that if Rivkah didn't come back with him, there would be a chance for his daughter.

Rashi doesn't mention this the first time Eliezer's statement appears because there the Torah says it with a *vav*. Only when Eliezer tells over the story of his journey to Besuel, when it's written without a *vav*, there *Rashi* comments because it could read as אֵלַי—to me, which hints at Eliezer's hidden intention.

---

1   See *Bereishis* 24:39.

Why would the Torah change the spelling? If this was the intention of Eliezer all along, then why isn't it spelled without the *vav* initially as well, especially if he's hoping that Avraham understand his truest desires?

I had a thought that perhaps can help us understand these *pesukim* and ourselves as well. There are times that we feel tremendously inspired, excited, and elevated. Maybe on Motza'ei Yom Kippur or after a fabulous shiur, we decide to make a sincere change in our lifestyle. Unfortunately, as time passes and the excitement dies down, we revert back to the way things were.

The word אוּלַי, written complete, became lacking without a *vav*. Not only was it lacking, but it took on a new meaning completely—to me. Other intentions, i.e., how this can benefit me, began creeping in.

Perhaps we can say that Eliezer originally had pure intentions, אוּלַי, and only later did the other thought come up, אֵלַי.

Sometimes, when young men and women enter the working world, they are very strong in their spiritual commitments. They don't compromise on what is truly important to their *neshamah*. Then, over time, things start to slowly slip away—both knowingly and unknowingly.

May we merit to keep our fire lit and to not allow it to die down with time. May we have pure intentions that remain that way as we forge ahead!

Toldos

CHOOSE TO INFUSE

וַיָּבֹא עֵשָׂו מִן הַשָּׂדֶה וְהוּא עָיֵף.

And Eisav came from the field,
and he was tired.
Bereishis 25:29

Rabbi Yissachar Frand pointed out that Eisav is the first one in the Torah to be called tired. What was he so tired from?

Chazal tell us that when Eisav returned from the fields, he had just committed the "Big Three," i.e., the three cardinal sins. This is what exhausted him and depleted him of his energy.

The opposite is true of those who learn Torah. We are taught that Torah weakens a person, however, the *Yerushalmi* states that Torah *lishmah*, Torah with pure intention, doesn't have a weakening effect on the individual learning. On the contrary! *Yeshayahu* teaches, "Those who hope in Hashem, will have renewed strength."[1] Spiritual endeavors won't weaken us, but they will give us a fresh and invigorating energy. They infuse us with a will to accomplish more. When we feel a sense of purpose, we are driven to accomplish more on our earthly mission.

---

1   *Yeshayahu* 40:31.

23

Chazal have so beautifully taught us that מִצְוָה גּוֹרֶרֶת מִצְוָה.[2] Each mitzvah lends us strength to accomplish the next mitzvah.

Rav Avraham Pam spoke at a *Siyum HaShas* and urged everybody to consider doing the *Daf* in the morning, because then your day becomes a "*Daf* day"! It fuels one to go forward in the day, looking for more opportunities to serve Hashem. It sets the tone for a *Daf*-style day, and it empowers the *Daf* learner to make choices that are aligned with the title of a "*Daf* guy."

With the guidance of my Rav, Rav Moshe Weinberger, this was something that I wanted to bring into my work day. My *chavrusa* and I, *baruch Hashem*, meet every morning before davening, and I can tell you firsthand that this has had an amazing *hashpa'ah* on the rest of my day. There is something special about learning before checking the emails and before the day gets so busy. A person has a clear mind at that time, and there are no distractions. For me (and many people I know who do the same), this is an invaluable way to begin one's day, and I strongly recommend it to you!

There are many stories told about our *tzaddikim* that indicate that not only did their physical weakness not impede their ability to learn; if anything, they were able to accomplish physically what astounded those around them.

As a young boy, Rav Elyashiv was sickly and unwell, and he required many medical treatments. However, as he aged, it was obvious that he needed very little food and very little sleep because his spiritual accomplishments gave him physical strength. Rav Yaakov Kaminetsky once stayed at a hotel and was asked by the woman cleaning the room if he knew "the really nice rabbi, Rabbi Yoel Teitelbaum." Rav Yaakov responded that of course he knew the Satmar Rebbe. She then went on to say, "That rabbi is the greatest and nicest. When he stayed in this hotel, I never had to make his bed. I came into his room each day, and the bed was already made for me!" Rav Yaakov smiled because he knew the secret—that the Satmar Rebbe never slept in his bed!

---

2   *Avos* 4:2.

Only Torah can give that level of supernatural strength to a person.

May we merit physical and spiritual strength to accomplish the spiritual goals that we set for ourselves each and every day.

JUST PASSING THROUGH

וַיִּתְרֹצֲצוּ הַבָּנִים בְּקִרְבָּה.

The children clamored within her.

Bereishis 25:22

The Midrash says that when Rivkah **stood** by the *beis midrash*, Yaakov pushed to go out. However, when she **passed** a house of idolatry, Eisav **ran** and pushed to get out.

The *Oznayim LaTorah* points out the difference between the two circumstances. The holy Rivkah stood outside the *beis midrash* but hurried past a house of idolatry. The children reacted differently as well. Yaakov only pushed, whereas Eisav ran and pushed. Yaakov didn't have to run because Rivkah was standing there, however, Eisav had to run because Rivkah was moving too fast past his place of interest, as she didn't want to be near such a place for a second longer than necessary.

The midrash is teaching us the importance of putting ourselves in spiritually productive environments. There are times that we must attend a holiday party, convention, or uncomfortable business meetings. Yes, we need to be there, but we should attempt to "pass by," i.e., do it as quickly as possible—not lingering more than necessary. Regarding holy settings, we should "stand" and soak in the surroundings.

There is the pull of Eisav and Yaakov within us at all times. We need to set ourselves up for success with the knowledge of how Eisav, the *mashal* for the *yetzer hara*, conducts himself. He doesn't just push—he runs! There is a real passion exhibited by Eisav as he tries to get out into the world. A Yaakov-style environment requires no running on our part. We need just a push to feel comfortable in that setting.

It is quite interesting that this *parashah* comes out during the time of the year when there are "holiday parties." Having been at many of these over the years, I see it's very easy to lose sight of why we really have to be there. There are plenty of opportunities to **pass** through and not **stand**.

The *Oznayim LaTorah* asks why Rivkah didn't just stay home so she wouldn't have to endure the inner turmoil taking place. He answers that had she remained at home, the two boys inside her would have killed each other. At least, when she left the house, she knew that one of them would be happy at any given time.

The solution in life is not to remain secluded and homebound so that we avoid outer world temptation. It would be self-destructive and could possibly lead to an implosion. We go out and choose to empower the Yaakov, the *tov* that is within, and make sure that "he" is always the happy one.

May we merit to stand by all holy endeavors and settings, and may we have the wisdom to know when to run past that which is calling us from the other side.

Vayeitzei

WATER FOR ONE AND ALL

וַיַּרְא וְהִנֵּה בְאֵר בַּשָּׂדֶה.

And he saw, and behold, there was a well
in the field.

Bereishis 29:2

Three strong and capable shepherds, who were used to manual labor, were unable to lift the rock off of the well. Along comes Yaakov Avinu and easily lifts the rock to uncover the water-filled well.

In *Tanach*, very often the Torah is compared to water. The thirst that one has for water is the thirst that one should ultimately have for Torah. And just as water travels to the lowest point, so too, Torah is made available for all people, on all levels.

The well that held the water was covered by a heavy rock. We too sometimes feel that the Torah we crave to learn and understand doesn't seem accessible or easy to attain. We are not alone. On Har Sinai, Moshe Rabbeinu went to learn Torah with Hashem Himself, but he kept on forgetting what he was taught. Chazal compare his situation to that of a shield that is covered in oil and fat so that enemy arrows slide right off. Only when Hashem gave Moshe Rabbeinu the gift of memory was he able to retain and pass to us the gift of Torah.

Torah is purely spiritual. Man is comprised of physical and spiritual, and the gift of Torah doesn't stick to the physicality of man, as oil and water can't mix. It needs to be a gift from Hashem so that our whole self can accept it. It's understandable that many people have a natural desire to spend hours in the office and not in front of a *sefer*. They may say, "I'm not cut out for it; it's not my thing; I'm the *chessed* kind of guy." It isn't natural for the body to appreciate Torah, but with a little bit of effort, we are given the gift. And what a rewarding outcome that is! We need to roll up our sleeves to roll off that rock, and once we do, we will taste the delicious waters that lie within the sea of Torah.

In *The Maggid Speaks*, Rabbi Paysach Krohn writes a story about Rav Shalom Schwadron who went to a certain town and delivered a speech on the topic of *chillul Shabbos*. Many in the town didn't appreciate the harsh and honest perspective, and they banned him from entering the town again. Rav Shalom went to discuss the matter with the Brisker Rav, because his intentions had been *l'shem Shamayim*, and he felt badly about what had transpired.

The Brisker Rav said, "Why do we make a *berachah* each morning לַעֲסוֹק בְּדִבְרֵי תוֹרָה—to be busy with Torah? Why don't we say לִלְמוֹד—to learn?" He answered, "If you were a carpet salesman trying to convince people to purchase your carpet, would you speak harshly to them? Would you put them down? Of course not! That would be counterproductive. Instead, you would make them feel great so that they will be more likely to buy your product. Torah should be treated like a business deal. You must put in the effort necessary and sweeten the deal so that those trying to attain it will work to lift the boulders and taste its sweetness."

When Rebbetzin Kanievsky was *niftar*, a generous man came to the *shivah* house. He approached Rav Chaim and said he wanted to write out a check to a worthy tzedakah organization for the *zechus* of the *neshamah* of the Rebbetzin. Rav Chaim told the man that he should instead learn half-an-hour each day for her *neshamah*. The man said, "Fine, but who should I write out the check to?" Again, Rav Chaim requested that he learn more, each day.

Of course, tzedakah is important; we need not explain that. However, Rav Chaim was teaching us that Torah isn't reserved for the bright ones while the others just write the checks. With effort, Torah is accessible to all. It is a deal that we can all get!

May we merit to discover the sweetness of Torah and dip our cups into the *be'er mayim chaim*. May the effort that we invest in removing our rocks reward us with the ultimate pleasure.

NO STONE UNTURNED

וַיִּפְגַּע בַּמָּקוֹם וַיָּלֶן שָׁם כִּי בָא הַשֶּׁמֶשׁ
וַיִּקַּח מֵאַבְנֵי הַמָּקוֹם וַיָּשֶׂם מְרַאֲשֹׁתָיו
וַיִּשְׁכַּב בַּמָּקוֹם הַהוּא.

And he arrived at the place and lodged there
because the sun had set, and he took from
the stones of the place and placed [them] at
his head, and he lay down in that place.

Bereishis 28:11

Rashi quotes the Midrash that states that Yaakov put the rocks around his head as protection from wild animals.

This seems rather strange. If Yaakov was truly concerned about the danger of wild animals, how would it help to surround his head and leave the rest of his body exposed to the elements?

I saw a simple yet powerful answer: Yaakov really wanted to gather all the stones that he could, as it says, "from the stones of the place," but of the stones that were there, he was only able to surround his head. Essentially, he did all that he could possibly do, as there were no more stones to be found. So while the protection was somewhat limited, he had put in the maximum effort that he could.

When we lock our doors, install security cameras and home alarm systems, do we produce a foolproof safety net? We know that it's not 100 percent, yet we did our part and Hashem will do His. Ultimately, all protection comes from Hashem, and yet we still do what we have to, knowing that it's only effort and not a guarantee.

Rav Chaim Kanievsky once told someone, "I work for *parnassah* two days a year: the first day of Rosh Hashanah and the second day!" Rav Chaim knows where it really comes from, and that is where he puts in work.

There was a Yid who managed to stay calm during a terrible financial time period when most other people were very nervous. When asked how he managed to act as such, he responded: "My market days are Rosh Hashanah."

Remembering how it all comes to us and Who it comes from helps us properly direct our strength and nerves.

Is it worth missing a minyan to get extra time in the office? Or to come home too late to see the kids? We need to collect our stones, put in the appropriate effort, and then rest assured in the knowledge that the *parnassah* comes from Hashem.

May we merit a life of *berachah* and of physical and financial security with Hashem as our true protector.

THE LOVE OF MY LIFE

וַיַּרְא ה' כִּי שְׂנוּאָה לֵאָה.

And Hashem saw that Leah was hated.

Bereishis 29:31

While there are numerous times that the Torah mentions the love that Yaakov had for Rachel, concerning Leah, the *pasuk* tells us that she was hated. How can this possibly be? Could Yaakov Avinu hate a fellow Jew, let alone his wife?! This needs to be explained.

A profound understanding of true love is revealed to us here: Yaakov Avinu loved Rachel! When there is deep love toward one thing, everything else is secondary. Yaakov had no negative feelings toward Leah; she was never put down. Instead, since Yaakov's truest love was reserved exclusively for Rachel, everything else was as if he hated it.

When we truly love someone or something, it is self-evident. It is what we talk about, what we think about, and what we are passionate about. Regardless of what we say, everyone will know what it is that we love. There are many people who spend the majority of their day at work, yet it is obvious that their love of Torah and mitzvos is what gives them their *chiyus*. One can sit in a *beis midrash* all day or give *shiurim* to *talmidim*, and yet that person's love and passion might be reserved for material pursuits and hobbies. What are we excited to talk about? Do our eyes twinkle when sharing a *gevaldike vort*? Or is our enthusiasm reserved for the latest news on rent control? Having other interests outside Torah is fine, but which is our true love? Our families don't need us to tell them what is important to us or what it is we love; they will know it when they see it!

My *rebbi* taught me that this lesson is part of the story of Chanukah: "רַבִּים בְּיַד מְעַטִּים"—the few Chashmona'im were able to overpower the many Yevanim. A little *kedushah*, i.e., what is truly *chashuv* to us, can overpower the mundane—even that which takes up much more of our time!

In reality, our *neshamah* is a *chelek* of Hashem; it knows what we love. It is the truest desire of every Jew to cling to Hashem. We don't always know what we truly want until we try it, but once we explore the beauty of Hashem and His Torah, we will fall in love.

Shlomo HaMelech writes, "וְאִישׁ לְפִי מַהֲלָלוֹ—A man is what he praises."[1] Our speech broadcasts to the world what it is that we truly feel strongly about.

When Hashem created man, the Torah says, "And He blew into his nostrils the soul of life,"[2] and the *Targum* says that this refers to the power of speech. Our words and inner self are really one.

Growing up, my friend's father would take him to a butcher shop. He doesn't remember how many salamis were hanging by the counter, but he does remember that the butcher was always excited to share "a good *vort*" with his father. He always had time for a good *peshat*, even when he was busy with customers. His smile and excitement were not reserved for a large meat order but for the joy of a *d'var Torah*.

May we merit giving our hearts over to the true love of our life—Hashem and His Torah.

---

1   *Mishlei* 27:21.
2   *Bereishis* 2:7.

Vayishlach

TO WALK THE WALK

עִם לָבָן גַּרְתִּי.

With Lavan I have lived.
Bereishis 32:5

Rashi tells us that the word *"garti"* has the same letters as the word *"taryag"*—the *gematria* of 613. The message that Yaakov was sending was that while he may have lived with Lavan the *rasha*, he didn't learn from his evil ways and continuously observed the 613 mitzvos. With this message, he was warning Eisav not to initiate war with him.

Rashi's words seem redundant, though. Once Yaakov states that he kept the 613 mitzvos, is it necessary to also state that he didn't learn from his evil ways?

Rabbi Yissachar Frand quotes Rav Yaakov Yitzchak Ruderman as saying that we see from here that it is possible for one to technically observe the mitzvos and yet be strongly lacking in their service of Hashem. Keeping mitzvos doesn't automatically lead to living as a better Jew. The Torah doesn't discuss or elaborate every life situation and scenario, or how we should conduct ourselves in each one. The Torah gives us general guidelines, and from those we must derive the true *ratzon Hashem*. Even learning *Toras Hashem* needs to be infused with awareness of *ratzon Hashem*.

A teenager once came to speak to Rabbi Moshe Weinberger. He was feeling dejected and was slowly drifting away. As they were talking, Rabbi Weinberger asked the boy if he learns Gemara every day. The boy responded in the affirmative. "And did you ever think about Hashem when learning Gemara?" Rabbi Weinberger asked him. The boy responded, "I was never told to do that!"

It is very nice to kiss the Torah as it passes us in shul, but does Hashem want us to elbow our way through the crowd to reach it? It is honorable to dress as a *ben* or *bas Torah*, but are we to judge others who don't do the same? When one grows to new heights in their *avodas Hashem*, is it *ratzon Hashem* to impose that on others? The Torah is *ein sof*; it has been here before us and will continue after us. The same is true of our fulfillment of it. It can't be limited to the specific, technical laws but needs to overflow into who we are and how we live.

The laws of Torah are called "halachah," which comes from the word *halichah*—walking. It serves as a guide to how we live each day. The word "Torah" means *l'horos*—to show. It shows us how to live so that we can become exalted and elevated people. If you had the opportunity to watch Rav Elyashiv or read about Rav Aryeh Levin, you can tangibly feel what Torah does to a *ben Adam*. When we enter our workplace, we have countless opportunities to walk as a Jew and to positively influence others around us. Each choice of what to look at and what not to look at, what to say and what not to say, what to hear and what to ignore...

Rabbi Ephraim Wachsman tells the story of a fellow who passed inappropriate signs on the way to work. He made a deal with himself that every time he doesn't look, he will set aside one dollar. After a while, he counted up the money. It was two thousand dollars! With that money, he bought a brand-new Menorah. How beautiful those lights must be!

May we all merit to use the halachos for our *halichos*, to walk in directions that are Torah directions and that lead us on the path of the righteous.

Vayeishev

PLAN B: THE PLAN FOR ME

וַיֵּשֶׁב יַעֲקֹב.

And Yaakov settled.

Bereishis 37:1

Rashi quotes the Midrash that says how after all of Yaakov Avinu's previous struggles, he was hoping to settle down in peace and tranquility. However, the anguish over the kidnapping of Yosef didn't allow him to do so. The Midrash then states, "Though the righteous seek calm and tranquility, Hashem says, 'Are the righteous not satisfied with what is prepared for them in the World to Come, but rather, they also want to dwell at ease in this world?'"

It is difficult to understand the error in Yaakov Avinu's reasoning. If he sought some peace after all that he had experienced, surely it was for the sake of having *menuchas ha'nefesh* to serve Hashem properly! If so, what was wrong with the request?

The Brisker Rav answers this question as follows: People assume that the ideal scenario is to serve Hashem without distraction. In reality, Hashem specifically prefers that people serve Him despite their worldly difficulties and preoccupations. This isn't implying that Hashem specifically wants difficulties for us, but rather that wherever Hashem puts us, and with whatever Hashem gives us, that is how we are supposed to serve Him. The physical situation that we find ourselves in is not a mistake but is part of Creation. When we encounter a bump in the road, it's not a mistaken obstacle but what we need. So often, when we find ourselves in a difficult situation, we say, "if only this wouldn't be happening, everything would be OK." That isn't the mindset that we should cultivate. Rather, we should say, "If Plan A isn't working out, Hashem wants us to grow through Plan B."

> *A talmid came to speak with his rebbi about his issues with anger. Mid-conversation, the rebbi asked the boy to leave the room and told him not to worry as they would continue speaking right after he speaks to his attendant. The talmid left the room, and the door was still partly opened so he could hear what was being said in the room. The talmid overheard his rebbi say, "My talmid waiting outside is working on his anger. I want to test him. Please let him know that I am not seeing anyone else for the rest of the day (although he had just told that student that he would continue with him). I would like to see his reaction."*
>
> *When the attendant walked out and told the talmid, he didn't get worked up or frustrated, but rather he smiled and responded, "OK, I will go home." Upon hearing the talmid's reaction, the rebbi called him back in and said, "From what I saw, you don't seem to have an anger issue. You handled yourself very well."*
>
> *The talmid responded, "Rebbi, I overheard you speaking with the attendant. It wasn't difficult to respond calmly because I knew that you were testing me!"*
>
> *The rebbi said, "Exactly! This is true with every life situation. Hashem orchestrates them all as life opportunities for growth. This is the test of life!"*

Adopting this method of viewing life's circumstances will make everything that much easier. Which occupation we choose, where our office is located, who our boss is, and who our employees are—all of it is exactly the setting that He wants us to serve Him in. (Of course, making the right choices in those areas that are under our control should be made according to the Torah.) If we find ourselves weighed down by work without as much time to learn, we can choose to serve Him then and there by doing the work honestly and *b'simchah*.

May we merit to live a life knowing that "there is no place void of God."[1] We should have a life filled with *avodas Hashem* in every situation in life that we find ourselves in.

---

1   *Zohar.*

Mikeitz

PUT YOUR MONEY WHERE YOUR MOUTH IS

וַיִּפְתַּח הָאֶחָד אֶת שַׂקּוֹ לָתֵת מִסְפּוֹא
לַחֲמֹרוֹ בַּמָּלוֹן וַיַּרְא אֶת כַּסְפּוֹ וְהִנֵּה
הוּא בְּפִי אַמְתַּחְתּוֹ.

And one opened his bag to give feed to his
donkey at the inn, and he saw his money,
and behold it was in the opening of his bag.

Bereishis 42:27

When the brothers opened their sacks and found the money, *Rashi* points out that it was Levi who found it in the mouth (opening) of the sack. The Malbim explains that while all the other *shevatim* only found their money later under the grain at the bottom of the sacks, Levi's money was at the mouth—the opening.

Levi would later be the only *shevet* not involved in the *avodah* of Mitzrayim. We also know that *shevet* Levi spent their days learning Torah; it was their only profession. The root of all material wealth comes from the blessing of Torah. That is why Levi was the first to see the money.

Right when Levi finds the money, he and his brothers say, "What is this that Hashem has done to us?" They immediately attributes it to Hashem. Where did Levi find the money? In the mouth of the sack. The mouth is a reference to the study of Torah. It is the words of Torah that flow from the lips of *shevet* Levi that brings them *berachah*.

While the Kohanim and the Leviim worked in the Beis Hamikdash, their sustenance was provided by the *terumos* and *maasros* from Klal Yisrael. In reality, it was the *avodah* in the Beis Hamikdash that generated *berachah* for everyone else.

My friend was fortunate enough to marry off his daughter to a fine young man who is presently learning in Kollel. When he closes a deal, he calls his son-in-law to thank him for supporting him. He truly believes that his son-in-law's sincere Torah learning brings *berachah* to his work.

The *Zohar* says that when we encounter a needy person and reach into our pockets to give him tzedakah, in reality, Hashem has just given us a gift on a golden platter. As we all know, the mitzvah of giving greatly outweighs the value of the money itself.

Rebbetzin Henny Machlis would often say, "If you have ten dollars and you give a poor man three, what are you left with?" Most would answer seven. She'd respond, "The truest answer is three! Who knows what you will do with the seven left? But the three that were used for the mitzvah you will have forever!"

May we always remember the importance of our "*peh*"—our mouth, as empowered by the Torah we speak and the mitzvos we do, because that is what truly carries and supports us. May we continue to "carry on" with *maasim tovim*.

Vayigash

YOU RULE!

וַיְשִׂימֵנִי לְאָב לְפַרְעֹה וּלְאָדוֹן לְכָל
בֵּיתוֹ וּמֹשֵׁל בְּכָל אֶרֶץ מִצְרָיִם.

He has made me as a father to Pharaoh,
master over his entire house, and a ruler in
all the land of Mitzrayim.

Bereishis 45:8

When Yosef reassures his brothers that they need not feel bad for sending him to Mitzrayim, he attributes what happened to Hashem alone and mentions the three places that Hashem had given him dominance over Mitzrayim:

1. Over Pharaoh
2. Over his household
3. Over his land

Rabbi Yissachar Frand asks why, when the brothers returned to Yaakov Avinu, all they said is that Yosef is the ruler of all of Egypt. Why did they omit the other two?

Rabbi Frand answers with the following *mashal*: A Yerushalmi Yid, who has never been out of Meah Shearim, has a son that goes off to university in America. After university, the son lands a job in a prestigious firm, and after many years of hard work, he climbs the ladder of success and ultimately becomes Chief of Staff at the White House. When he reunites with his father after many years being apart, his father has only one question for him: "Did you, my precious son, remain a real Yid, a sincere Jew? Or did the high echelons of society get the best of you?" Instead of being concerned with his son's financial success and prestige, the father is more concerned that his son had an encounter with his tefillin than whether he had an encounter with the President. Did he remain honest and faithful? Or was he blinded by his position of power?

What does it mean to rule over Mitzrayim? Mitzrayim is equated with the *yetzer hara* trying to mask Hashem, as Pharaoh said, "Who is Hashem?" Mitzrayim was a place of hard work without purpose, where the structures that the Jews built sank in quicksand. It was a place devoid of higher purpose and *tachlis*. To be *moshel* meant to rise above and have control over the *tumah* of Mitzrayim that you may find yourself in.

All that mattered to Yaakov Avinu was that his son, Yosef HaTzaddik, remained an *ehrliche Yid*. That is why the *shevatim* only said, "וְכִי הוּא מֹשֵׁל בְּכָל אֶרֶץ מִצְרָיִם."[1] He was *zocheh* to rule over Mitzrayim, the *yetzer hara*, and the negative environment.

May we all be *zocheh* to find the strength to be *moshel* over our personal Mitzrayim. As we taste the sweetness of success, may it be true success—that which a Yiddishe parent would only want for their child.

---

1   *Bereishis* 45:26.

Vayechi

FROM THE VALLEY I CALL OUT

יְשִׂמְךָ אֱלֹקִים כְּאֶפְרַיִם וְכִמְנַשֶּׁה.

May God make you like Ephraim
and Menasheh.
Bereishis 48:20

Why specifically are Ephraim and Menasheh chosen to be the source of a blessing for the future Klal Yisrael?

First, the *Midrash Mordechai* points out that while all the other pairs of brothers had specific issues between them (Kayin and Hevel, Yitzchak and Yishmael, Yaakov and Eisav, Yosef and the *shevatim*), by this pair of brothers there were no issues. There was no jealousy when Menasheh, the older of the two, saw that Yaakov Avinu placed his right hand, i.e., the stronger hand, on the younger brother. In fact, Yaakov also used Ephraim's name first for the *berachah* that would be repeated for years to come!

Second, these two were unique in that they were the only ones to be born and raised in Mitzrayim, a land full of immorality and *tumah*. The other *shevatim*, on the other hand, all lived amongst each other in Canaan. Only Ephraim and Menasheh knew what it meant to attain *gadlus* despite the negative environments one may be surrounded by.

Furthermore, says the *Midrash Mordechai*, even in a healthy and positive environment, the younger generation slowly moves further away from *kedushah*—נִתְקַטְּנוּ הַדּוֹרוֹת. Yet, Ephraim and Menasheh broke that rule. The *pasuk* states, "כִּרְאוּבֵן וְשִׁמְעוֹן יִהְיוּ לִי";[1] they were just like Reuven and Shimon from the previous generation. They were able to defy the expected descent of the generation and maintain a high level of purity.

From where did they build such strength of character and this resilient nature? From their father Yosef HaTzaddik, of course. Despite his terrible circumstances, being mistreated by his brothers, and being wrongfully thrown into prison, the Torah tells us that the name of Hashem was constantly on his lips. As a result of this, he became an "אִישׁ מַצְלִיחַ"—a successful man.[2] It was so obviously visible on Yosef that even his master Potiphar saw that Hashem was with him.

Yosef HaTzaddik had the extraordinary ability to see the *yad Hashem* under the most trying circumstances, and this is the *chinuch* that they absorbed from a very young age. There was no jealousy between them because Hashem's role in their lives was at the forefront of their minds, and they didn't see their accomplishments as their own. There was no נִתְקַטְּנוּ הַדּוֹרוֹת because of their ability to see Hashem despite the many advances that came with each new generation. Yosef taught his family that "בִּלְעָדָי—it is not me,"[3] and when he could have taken credit as the interpreter of dreams, he told Pharaoh, "It isn't me; it's God."

We all have spiritual safe havens in our life—our shul, our *beis midrash*, and hopefully our homes. Yet, very often, we are out in the world of Mitzrayim—the world of *avodah*, far away from our spiritual source. While we may not be getting whipped, each day comes with its own slew of *nisyonos* that are uniquely presented at work. It's much harder to relate to those *nisyonos* as *avodas ha'kodesh*. The *yetzer hara* keeps presenting himself on our screens, and yet we can be *matzliach*! Take Hashem to the office; view your computer screen as a tool that

---

1   *Bereishis* 48:5.

2   Ibid. 39:2.

3   Ibid. 41:16.

will elevate you. Consider your commute as a trip that will bring you closer to your Creator. Through Mitzrayim, we can attain a level that not everyone is *zocheh* to.

As we bring our children to the *bris milah*, the *Targum Yonasan* says that we bless them with this *berachah*, "Be like Ephraim and Menasheh." At the onset of a Jewish boy's life, we bentch him that he realizes how every moment has such opportunity, even when all seems dark. He can set the clock back and be as great as the previous generations!

Sefer
Shemos

Shemos

WORK MORE, MAKE MORE?

וַיְצַו פַּרְעֹה בַּיּוֹם הַהוּא אֶת הַנֹּגְשִׂים
בָּעָם וְאֶת שֹׁטְרָיו לֵאמֹר לֹא תֹאסִפוּן
לָתֵת תֶּבֶן לָעָם לִלְבֹּן הַלְּבֵנִים
כִּתְמוֹל.

And Pharaoh commanded on that day...
don't continue to give them straw...

Shemos 5:6–7

Pharaoh was infuriated by Moshe's attempt to take us out of Mitzrayim and B'nei Yisrael's lackadaisical attitude toward their work. He decided to push them even harder, to their breaking point, by imposing upon them their daily quota without giving them any material.

The obvious question is why Pharaoh would impose harsher work requirements that didn't serve any benefit to him at all. It made B'nei Yisrael work harder to find straw just to keep up with what they were already producing! Wouldn't it have made more sense to just raise the quota? Pharaoh would gain while also causing the Jews to work harder—a win-win for him!

The Torah is teaching us that the generally accepted notion of "working harder equals producing more" is not necessarily true. Pharaoh

49

was the leader of Mitzrayim, a word that translates as "narrowness," a narrow point of view, an inability to see the larger picture. This sort of thinking can cause us to burn the midnight oil, redouble our work efforts, and yet produce nothing extra.

There is a reasonable amount of time and effort that each individual can put into his work, each using his wisdom and Torah guidance. When we step out of our narrow space and acknowledge that, ultimately, our *parnassah* comes from Hashem, then we can lock up and go home when the time arrives; we can also shut off our phones when it comes time to daven and for family time, as well.

When the *Ohr Hachaim Hakadosh* was Rav in Morocco, he instituted a three-day work week. The rest of the week was for Torah study. Suprisingly, it "worked out" very well, and the community flourished. When the *Ohr Hachaim* moved to Eretz Yisrael, the people in Morocco slowly began adding days to the work week until they found themselves working six days a week. However, they realized that their financial situation hadn't grown along with their added work days; rather, they still made the same amount as before!

The Gemara relates a fascinating event that took place in the time of the Beis Hamikdash. The Shiloach stream would issue a stream of water the size of a small coin (an *issur* coin). The king commanded that the hole be widened to allow for a stronger flow of water, but, much to his dismay, the change had the opposite effect and brought the water to a diminished flow. He reversed his decree, and it flowed as it had originally.[1] The Gemara then stated that this was a fulfillment of the words in *Yirmiyahu*, "Let the wise man not praise himself for his wisdom, nor the strong man praise himself for his strength."[2]

May we merit living with the knowledge that blessing **flows** according to the will of Hashem. It isn't always obviously seen, but He gave us clear directives on how to "tap" into the stream of blessing.

---

1   *Arachin* 10b.
2   *Yirmiyahu* 9:22.

Va'eira

THERE'S NO PLACE LIKE HOME

וַיִּפֶן פַּרְעֹה וַיָּבֹא אֶל בֵּיתוֹ.

*And Pharaoh turned and he came
to his house.*

Shemos 7:23

I t seems that the *pasuk*'s goal is to inform us that even after
makkas *dam*, Pharaoh didn't pay heed and remained unchanged.
Why then, does the *pasuk* say that "he turned and came home"? Why is
this necessary information?

The *Sifsei Tzaddik* says that although וַיִּפֶן means "to turn away," it also
means "to face." With this understanding, the *pasuk* is telling us that
once Pharaoh faced the situation, the truth became clear and he realized what he needed to do. He had to let the Jews go.

However, we know that it took another nine *makkos* for change to
take place! Nevertheless, the Torah is teaching us an impactful lesson:
a good thought is special and meaningful in the eyes of Hashem. Of
course, our goal is to follow up with the next step, but there is *chashivus*
given to even a good thought.

Rav Chaim Stein would often stress that Chazal say, "It is our will to
do Your Will, but the yeast in the dough (*yetzer hara*) holds us back."

Chazal are teaching us that our good will and desire, even before any action or success, are a high level unto themselves.

Getting back to Pharaoh: What happened when he had a good thought? Why couldn't he actualize it?

The *pasuk* ends off and says that "he came to his house." What house did he return to? A house of *avodah zarah* and *tumah*. He lived in a home of impurity and emptiness.

Our strength comes from our home. Our innermost desires can be actualized when we have a home that is focused on *avodas Hashem*, where a husband and wife desire to live an elevated life. We can act upon our good thoughts and exciting ideas when we come home to a family that emphasizes and strengthens these ideas as well. We are sometimes limited in our workplace environment. However, we can choose what our home environment is like. By creating a home with a foundation of Torah ideals and values, we will allow that home to foster tremendous growth and change.

There was tremendous excitement for all of the boys in yeshiva as they headed out on a bus for a long-awaited trip to a water park. It had been a long z'man, and they couldn't wait to enjoy the refreshing rides with their friends and teachers. The school had rented out the park for the day, and now that day had finally come. When the bus pulled up, it became clear within a matter of minutes that something was wrong. It seemed as though there had been a double booking because the park was already occupied by a girl's school. The buses would have to turn around and reschedule for another day.

The boys were unbelievably disappointed when the reality of their situation sunk in. One boy in the seventh grade stood up and yelled out to all of his friends, "We need to be happy, and we need to be grateful that we have an opportunity to keep Hashem's mitzvah. If we're not going into the water park because Hashem doesn't want us going, let us sing Ashreinu. We are so fortunate that we get to keep His mitzvos!" With that, this young boy broke out into song and dance. As his excitement spread through the bus, the mood changed and the boys were dancing like they've never danced before.

When the boys returned back to yeshiva, their rebbi ran eagerly to the principal's office to let him know what had transpired and that he had such a special boy in his class. The principal was completely amazed, and told the rebbi that another one of the buses had done the same thing. The rebbi was equally amazed when the principal told him that it was this boy's younger brother who led the boys in song and dance on the other bus. The principal called their home to ask their parents what the secret of their chinuch was, as clearly this home was special and unique. Their father told the principal the following story:

"A short time ago, my wife needed to do errands that the children were not interested in participating in. It would mean schlepping from store to store in the heat, going in and out of taxis—not fun. To appease the children, my wife told them that when they are ready to return home, she would purchase ices from the grocery store that they could all enjoy in the taxi. It did the trick! As the children followed their mother around town, they eagerly anticipated the refreshing treat that they would shortly enjoy. When they were almost finished at the grocery store, my wife picked out delicious looking ices and purchased them along with everything else. They got into the taxi, ripped open the packaging, and only then realized that the hechsher on the ices was not a hechsher that they trusted. Yes, the ices were kosher, but our family is careful and very specific when it comes to the foods that we eat. The children were crestfallen, but my wife explained to them lovingly that they were doing the right thing, and she would make sure that there would be a treat for them when they got home. They were all happy as she told them, 'Ashreinu! How fortunate we are to follow the will of Hashem!'

"She called me from the car and asked me to pick up a treat for when they returned home. When I heard what had happened, I told the children that one treat simply would not do and that I was going to set the table with candy and special treats and throw an Ashreinu party like they had never seen before. That is what we did. Perhaps that is why my boys responded as such today."

Let us never underestimate the power of the home!

May we merit that wherever we are, we always stay connected to home. The ideals, values and hashkafic foundations that we lay at home should carry us wherever we go.

THE ULTIMATE ENERGY BAR

וְלֹא שָׁמְעוּ אֶל מֹשֶׁה מִקֹּצֶר רוּחַ
וּמֵעֲבֹדָה קָשָׁה.

And they did not listen to Moshe from
shortness of breath and hard work.

Shemos 6:9

B'nei Yisrael were given the news that they'd anticipated
for so many years, and yet they were unable to enthusiasti-
cally respond.

Rabbi Moshe Meir Weiss says that the reason that B'nei Yisrael were
unable to respond to the ecstatic news was because they had not yet
received the gift of the Torah.

Nothing is more draining than useless, purposeless work. What gives
us strength? Purpose! Seeing and knowing that ultimately there is
a goal and a mission allows us to get through dark tunnels. Seeing this
shining light at the end of the tunnel infuses us, invigorates us, and
allows us to do more and to do better.

There are specific lines of work that make it easier to feel a sense of
purpose, such as healing people or keeping people safe. What can we do
when our job doesn't seem as lofty or purposeful in a meaningful way?

We all live with holiness. We raise families, pay yeshiva tuition, make Yom Tov, give tzedakah, and so on. The money we use for holy endeavors needs a conduit to reach us. With incredible *hashgachah*, Hashem gave us a job that allows us to bring more *berachah* and *kedushah* to His world. All jobs, within the confines of the Torah, are holy. They are the conduit to allow Hashem's *berachah* to be given to us.

"יְגִיעַ כַּפֶּיךָ כִּי תֹאכֵל אַשְׁרֶיךָ וְטוֹב לָךְ—You who eat by your handiwork are praised, and it is good for you..."[1] We follow God's plan by tapping into the resources He designates for us.

> The Megaleh Amukos, zt"l, let the people of Krakow know that he no longer wanted to be their Rav, but he didn't tell them the reason for his decision. Despite their many pleas that he would change his mind and stay with them, he remained firm in his decision. With a heavy heart, the community prepared a seudas p'reidah—goodbye party for the Megaleh Amukos. At the celebration, the Megaleh Amukos announced that he would continue serving as the Rav of Krakow. The community was shocked and overjoyed simultaneously, but they wanted to know (a) why he initially wanted to leave, and (b) what caused his change of heart to remain with the kehillah?
>
> The Megaleh Amukos said, "I still won't tell you why I wanted to leave, but I will tell you why I decided to stay: A very unusual din Torah came to me. A wealthy person saw a pauper selling bread and bagels on the sidewalk, and he said to him, "I recognize you from years back! You are a great talmid chacham! It isn't fitting for you to sell bread on the sidewalk. I will give you as much as you need to live each month so that you can learn Torah all day long in the beis midrash." The pauper agreed to the generous offer. Some time passed, and the wealthy person found the pauper again on the street selling bread and bagels. "We have an agreement," the wealthy man said, "why are you here?" The pauper answered that he and his wife decided to

---

1   *Tehillim* 128:2.

go back to their previous lifestyle, earning their living by selling bread on the street corners. "But why? Isn't it better to earn your parnassah easily so that you can learn Torah? And besides, you can't back down from an agreement without my consent," the wealthy man added. "We had an agreement, and a deal is a deal!"

They decided to ask the Megaleh Amukos, who asked the pauper, "Why don't you agree to this arrangement?" The pauper replied, "Before I received this generous stipend, my wife and I would wake up in the morning and immediately turn to Hashem, pleading that He help us earn a living. When we ground the wheat kernels, we prayed that the bread would be white and clean. When we kneaded the dough, we prayed that it should rise well. We also prayed that I should find dry logs to heat the oven (as fresh wood smokes and ruins the bread). We prayed that the bread should bake well, that people should buy it from us, and that they should be satisfied with their purchases so that they will buy from us again. When things went the way we wished, we praised Hashem for His kindness. From the beginning of the day until the end, we were constantly communicating and connecting to Hashem. But all of this stopped abruptly when we began receiving a monthly stipend. We weren't turning to Hashem anymore, because we knew that we will have everything we need. My wife and I decided that we don't want to live that way. We prefer going back to our old lifestyle because then Hashem will always be on our mind and in our prayers."

The Megaleh Amukos then said to the community, "After this din Torah, I decided that I wanted to remain here, in this city, to be among such Yidden!"

Our inner essence—our נְשָׁמָה—has a *gematria* of 395, the same as פַּרְנָסָה. My friend, Rav Yirmi Ginsburg, pointed this out to me. We see how there is a soul connection of man to his occupation.

What is it that serves as the beacon of light and inspiration to live with this knowledge and sense of purpose? The Torah! It is the greatest representation of Hashem in this world. Just as a monthly work meeting keeps us focused on our goals, a daily dose of Torah can keep us focused on our life goals.

May we merit to have lives filled with awakening moments. These moments will wake us up to see how holy each day truly is and give us renewed strength as we go *me'chayil el chayil*!

Bo

"BRING HASHEM TO WORK" WEEK

וַיֹּאמֶר ה' אֶל מֹשֶׁה בֹּא אֶל פַּרְעֹה כִּי
אֲנִי הִכְבַּדְתִּי אֶת לִבּוֹ וְאֶת לֵב עֲבָדָיו
לְמַעַן שִׁתִי אֹתֹתַי אֵלֶּה בְּקִרְבּוֹ.

Hashem said to Moshe, "Come to Pharaoh,
for I have hardened his and his servants'
hearts in order to increase my signs
among them."

Shemos 10:1

There is an obvious question that many *mefarshim* ask in regard to this very first *pasuk*, namely the Torah's use of the expression "come to Pharaoh" when telling Moshe to **go** to Pharaoh?

Perhaps one of the lessons gleaned from this is knowing that wherever we go, Hashem is there. Even when going to the lowliest of places, places that seem devoid of spirituality, you are able to come into the presence of Hashem. There is no place devoid of Him.

Rav Yitzchak Hutner once guided a young man who was preparing to leave yeshiva and go out into the workforce. The young man asked how he should deal with the fact that he would now be leading a double life. Rav Hutner responded that working and being a Torah Jew should not be considered leading a double life but should be viewed as leading a *broad* life—comparable to two different rooms in the same house. One must take his spiritual life with him when he enters the workplace.

> *One of the Chafetz Chaim's students was Reb Elya. A wealthy person once said to Reb Elya, "I am certain that I will always be wealthy."*
>
> *"Why are you so certain?" Reb Elya asked him. "Things change. Businesses collapse. It happens all the time…"*
>
> *"That's true," the wealthy man conceded, "however, my money isn't invested in one business. I have many businesses. Even if one or two of my businesses fail, many others can prosper. That's why I'm certain I will always be wealthy."*
>
> *"Don't say that," Reb Elya rebuked him. "There are no guarantees. Chazal say that parnassah is like a wheel. Sometimes one goes up, and sometimes one goes down." The wealthy man laughed because he was confident that his success would be forever.*
>
> *Reb Elya met with that wealthy person years later, but by then, he wasn't wealthy anymore. "You were right," the man said to Reb Elya.*
>
> *"What happened?" Reb Elya asked.*
>
> *The man replied, "In the good old days, I owned a bridge. I took a toll from everyone who crossed it, and that was one of my sources of income. Once, a brigade from Czar Nikolai's army was crossing the bridge with their cavalry and heavy equipment. The bridge collapsed, soldiers drowned in the river below, and there was a great loss of money, too. I knew that I had to escape. I rushed home, grabbed my financial documents so that I would still possess proof of my wealth and assets, and I quickly crossed the border. Soon after, I realized that I took the wrong documents. Everything was left behind. I've been poor ever since."*

Reb Elya had understood all along what this man unfortunately learned the hard way. If we do not include Hashem and make Him an equal partner in all our endeavors, we are most likely heading for failure.

A friend of mine does something very beautiful. When he starts a deal, he says that if it goes through, a certain percent of it will go to tzedakah. He really connects his work and his true goal.

May we merit to bring Hashem with us to the office and know that regardless of where we go, we are able to come closer to Him on our journey.

Beshalach

HEAVEN SENT

וְלֹא הֶעְדִּיף הַמַּרְבֶּה וְהַמַּמְעִיט
לֹא הֶחְסִיר.

Whoever took more had nothing extra,
and whoever took less was not lacking.

Shemos 16:18

The *mann* was a miraculous food on so many levels. One of the fascinating qualities that it possessed was that it became exactly the serving size that you needed. Regardless of how much or how little you took, it would grow or diminish to suit your family's needs.

The *Alshich Hakadosh* explains that this is exactly how the miracle of *parnassah* works as well. Even if we clock in overtime and spend late nights at the office, i.e., more than what is appropriate, we will still only make exactly what is destined for us. On Rosh Hashanah, Hashem decides what our income for the year will be save for a few exceptions, such as money spent on Torah, Shabbos and Yom Tov.

In addition, we know that "man was created to toil," while what we toil in is up to us to choose.

Therefore, if a person doesn't work or doesn't toil in Torah, he hasn't done his part to earn the gift of *parnassah*. If there is *ameilus*, there will be what Hashem planned for him. If he chooses to not overdo it at work and spend more time working over a Gemara, the outcome will still be the *parnassah* set for him. *Rashi* quotes Chazal that says: "שֶׁתִּהְיוּ עֲמֵלִים בַּתּוֹרָה—you should toil in Torah."

Just as the *mann* sustained us in the *midbar*, our *parnassah* sustains us now. Just as each person needed to put in effort to collect their *mann*, we put in our effort for our paycheck. The effort that one exerted to receive the *mann* was in direct relation to the level the person was on. The greater he was, the less exertion was necessary for him to receive his portion. So too, the more *ameilus* that we put into our *ruchniyus* labor, the less physical labor we'll need to collect our bounty.

> *A group of yeshiva boys in Eretz Yisrael decided to arrange an uplifting Shabbos in the North. It would be a way for them to unwind and recharge with niggunim, divrei Torah, and Shabbos ruach with a change of scenery. Each boy interested in coming was asked to contribute a specific amount to cover the costs of the Shabbaton.*
>
> *Reuven was approached, yet hesitated when asked if he was interested in participating. While there was nothing that excited him more, he had very little money and didn't know if it would be responsible for him to go without being certain he could pay his part. He then remembered a Gemara that he had learned that stated that one's parnassah is decided on Rosh Hashanah, with the exception of money spent on Shabbos, Yom Tov, and Torah learning. With that being the case, this would be money for Shabbos. He answered in the affirmative and pushed the matter out of his mind. Shabbos was beautiful, and it was as uplifting and elevating as he had expected.*
>
> *Sunday morning, as the money was being collected, Reuven asked if he can have a little more time as he contemplated where he would get the 388 shekalim and 60 agurot that came out as each boy's share. When he came to his dorm room, there was a letter from his parents sitting on his bed. It was a birthday card, which read: "We are presenting you with a birthday gift in the amount of one of every bill and coin of*

> *Israeli currency—200, 100, 50, and 20 NIS bills; 10, 5, 2, and*
> *1 NIS coins; and 50 and 10 agurot coins." All together, the gift*
> *totaled exactly 388 shekalim and 60 agurot!!!*

Sometimes, our portion of *mann* falls from the sky, sometimes it is deposited directly into our account, and sometimes it comes as a birthday gift.

May we merit to taste the sweetness of the *mann*—a heavenly taste. And just as the *mann* satiated each person completely, may we feel satiated with the *parnassah* that Hashem sends our way.

RIGHT TO THE SOURCE

וְנַחְנוּ מָה לֹא עָלֵינוּ תְלֻנֹּתֵיכֶם
כִּי עַל ה׳.

What are we? Not against us are your
complaints, but against Hashem.

Shemos 16:8

Moshe Rabbeinu's response seems out of character when he responds, "What are we? Do not come and complain to me. Take it up with Hashem!!" This is the response of *Rabban shel Yisrael*? Later, Moshe Rabbeinu said, "מְחֵנִי נָא מִסִּפְרְךָ—Erase me from your *sefer*!" He always put his neck out for B'nei Yisrael. What is happening here?

The Tolna Rebbe, explaining Rabbeinu Bachya, says that in the *zechus* of the Jewish People saying, "**Zeh Keili v'anveihu**," at the time of *k'rias Yam Suf*, they were rewarded with the *mann*, of which the *pasuk* says, "**Zeh ha'davar**." What is the connection? The Tolna Rebbe explains that the *trup*—cantillation on the word "**Keili**" is on the "**Li**"—that he is **my** God. When a person is able to see and emphasize that not only is Hashem the Master of the universe but that He provides for Me—my needs, down to every last penny that I possess—he can tap into the "**zeh**" of the *mann*, the *matanah* that is so clearly *min ha'Shamayim*.

Rabbi Yissachar Frand explains that this is precisely why Moshe Rabbeinu responded in this surprising fashion. He was reminding B'nei Yisrael that they are capable of having a direct relationship with Hashem, and so they don't need to depend on Moshe Rabbeinu as their intermediary. The "*zeh*," according to Chazal, is used when we can point to something in a very tangible way. Moshe Rabbeinu was teaching B'nei Yisrael and not finding an excuse. To the extent that we believe this with sincerity, that Hashem is My God, He will be here for us and act in kind.

There is an amazing Midrash that explains that "*Va'yehi be'shalach Pharaoh…*" is hinting to some level of pain and sadness, as we know is the case whenever the expression of "*va'yehi*" is used. What pain was Pharoah experiencing? The loss of his relationship with Hashem. Now that B'nei Yisrael were leaving, he was losing whatever relationship he had with the Master of the universe. How shocking! We know that his relationship consisted of harsh *makkos* and difficult warnings. Yet, a relationship with the *Borei Olam* to whatever degree it is acquired is still a relationship. He was mourning the loss of even that!

May we be *zocheh* that as we say these words daily to always see that the Creator of the world is **my** Creator who is specifically involved in **my** life and **my** *mann* (i.e., **my** *parnassah*). May our relationship with Him feel personal and meaningful in the most positive of ways, and in that *zechus* He will, iy"H, unlock all the *berachah* that He has in store for us.

Yisro

TWENTY-TWENTY VISION

וְאֵת שְׁנֵי בָנֶיהָ אֲשֶׁר שֵׁם הָאֶחָד
גֵּרְשֹׁם כִּי אָמַר גֵּר הָיִיתִי בְּאֶרֶץ
נָכְרִיָּה.
וְשֵׁם הָאֶחָד אֱלִיעֶזֶר כִּי אֱלֹקֵי אָבִי
בְּעֶזְרִי וַיַּצִּלֵנִי מֵחֶרֶב פַּרְעֹה.

The name of one was Gershom, because he
said, "I was a stranger in a foreign land."
And the name of one was Eliezer, because
the God of my father was my savior, and he
saved me from the sword of Pharaoh.

Shemos 18:3–4

Moshe Rabbeinu chose names that symbolized the experiences he had gone through. That being the case, shouldn't the older son be named Eliezer, as Moshe was saved from the sword of Pharaoh before he was a stranger in a strange land? And secondly, being a stranger doesn't sound like a praise; it sounds more like a complaint?!

Rav Moshe Feinstein beautifully answers in the following way: when Moshe Rabbeinu said "I was a stranger," he was praising and thanking Hashem that he was able to stay as a "visitor" in the land of Midyan.

The Midyanim would have happily appointed Moshe to a high position of leadership, and yet Moshe remained who he was and didn't allow himself to become a Midyanite. With this, we can answer the first question, as well.

Moshe Rabbeinu was happy to have been saved from Pharaoh's grip. However, the only purpose of him being saved would be if he could remain on the same level, even in Midyan. If he were to become one of them, what purpose was there in being saved? Celebrating salvation is shortsighted until we know that we fulfill exactly what the purpose of life is for with our lives.

A Holocaust survivor once said that he couldn't understand why he was saved when so many others were brutally murdered. Why celebrate life? Only many years later, when he saw the Yiddishe children, grandchildren, and great grandchildren that were living an elevated Torah life and impacting others to do the same, was he truly capable of celebrating the salvation he had experienced many years earlier.

When we enter our workplace, even if we've taken the LIRR to Manhattan daily for the past twenty years, we should still feel like a stranger in a strange place. "This isn't my place; it isn't my comfort zone." There are times that we are obligated to attend certain work events that are not in the spirit of Torah. How do we feel when we are there? Do we feel like a *ger*? Do we feel strange and uncomfortable? Or do we find ourselves tapping to the beat as we move comfortably through the crowds?

A young man who had recently entered the work force called Rabbi Yissachar Frand with a complaint. He felt so uncomfortable with the environment he was in. The constant barrage of *nisyonos* that were so different than what he was used to in yeshiva. Rabbi Frand responded to his concern, "I give you a *berachah* that you should always feel exactly what you are feeling now!"

May we merit to feel like dwellers in our *ruchnius* lives and visitors in our *gashmius* lives.

Mishpatim

AN ACQUIRED TASTE

וְאֵלֶּה הַמִּשְׁפָּטִים אֲשֶׁר
תָּשִׂים לִפְנֵיהֶם.

And these are the judgments that you
should place before them.

Shemos 21:1

All of the 613 mitzvos can be divided into the two categories of *chok* and *mishpat*. *Mishpatim* are defined as laws that seem logical—our internal moral sense would dictate them even without the Torah. Some that fall into this category would be not to steal, not to kill, etc. *Chukim*, on the other hand, are the laws that we would never think of by using our own *sechel*, such as *shaatnez*, shaking a lulav on Sukkos, etc.

Against this rubric, how would you think *kibud av v'em* would be classified? Your parents have done so much for you, so it seems natural to honor them and thus it's a *mishpat*, no? Yet, concerning this mitzvah, the *Daas Zekeinim* says that it too is a *chok*! What does he mean by that? Which part of the mitzvah of honoring parents isn't logical? Many cultures across the globe adhere to some sort of generational honor system!

The *Daas Zekeinim* is teaching us a fundamental lesson on knowledge and logic. Even our logic, which is a Godly creation, has its limits. We will never be able to use human knowledge to "know better." We would naturally assume that it is more sincere to do mitzvos because "it just feels right," as opposed to "because that's what the Torah says." However, that isn't the strongest way of serving Hashem. Of course, when one is struggling with *emunah*, initially he may need sensible understanding. But once we have a deep-rooted understanding that *chochmas Hashem* and *chochmas haTorah* is superior, then our personal feelings and understanding can **enhance** our observance, but not **create** our observance.

> *A doctor once told his Rav that everyone was going to his competitor and thus he wasn't making a living. The Rav gave him this advice: "When someone calls for an appointment, tell him that the only slot open is in three months from now. People will then talk about how busy you are, and you will give off the impression of being a very sought-after doctor. This will cause your reputation to soar." The doctor followed this advice and was very successful. One day, the Rav needed medical attention and he called the doctor for an appointment. The doctor told the Rav that the only slot available was in three months. The Rav replied: "Are you going to play this game with me? I'm the one who taught it to you. I'm the one who made you successful!"*

As we see from this parable, the logic of *Hakadosh Baruch Hu* supersedes human knowledge, and we can strengthen ourselves and remind ourselves constantly of who created the mitzvos and all that we are obligated in. We will find the most success by following His 613 pieces of advice.

Certain foods are extremely unhealthy. If you are mindful of your health, you will stop eating products that are detrimental to your body. Although nothing is more tempting to the senses than a hotdog with French fries, you resist the temptation because your health is more important. This is the first step—reacting to a fact instead of your "gut" feeling. After some time, you lose your desire for foods made with preservatives and coloring, and it becomes somewhat repulsive to you. You begin to "feel in your gut" that you don't enjoy it. This is the second step—when your mind and body, or your logic and emotion, begin to work in sync.

David HaMelech says, "Teach me the reasons and logic of Your Torah, because I have belief in You."[1] Why does David HaMelech say **because** of *emunah*; shouldn't it be in order to acquire *emunah*? The answer is that we must accept what Hashem tells us, whether or not we understand, and only after we enhance our understanding and educate ourselves in the *taamei ha'mitzvos*—literally, the "flavors" of the commandments. We then work on developing our feelings to the point that we desire Hashem's desires.

It can seem logical to miss the minyan if we need more time to finish a work project. It would seem acceptable to mingle at the meeting more than necessary as it will help us financially. It's the "*parnassah heter*" that we sometimes give ourselves. The logic that we think is necessary to help us advance. The most objective truth is our *chukim* and *mishpatim*, and by following the Torah's rules of *parnassah* etiquette, we will always be a success.

May we merit adhering to the 613 mitzvos and learning deeper and more meaningful layers of understanding with each passing day. In this way, we will feel an inner harmony with what we do and why we do it!

---

1   *Tehillim* 119:66.

Terumah

DO I MEASURE UP?

וְעָשׂוּ אֲרוֹן עֲצֵי שִׁטִּים אַמָּתַיִם
וָחֵצִי אָרְכּוֹ וְאַמָּה וָחֵצִי רָחְבּוֹ וְאַמָּה
וָחֵצִי קֹמָתוֹ.

They shall make an ark of acacia wood,
two-and-a-half cubits its length, a cubit-
and-a-half its width, and a cubit-and-a-half
its height.

Shemos 25:10

וְעָשִׂיתָ שֻׁלְחָן עֲצֵי שִׁטִּים אַמָּתַיִם
אָרְכּוֹ וְאַמָּה רָחְבּוֹ וְאַמָּה וָחֵצִי קֹמָתוֹ.

And you shall make a table of acacia wood,
two cubits its length, one cubit its width,
and a cubit-and-a-half its height.

Shemos 25:23

The *Aron* represents Torah, as it contains the *Luchos* within it, and the *Shulchan* represents *parnassah*, as a table connotes one's sustenance. Perhaps there is a lesson that can be taken from the measures of these two holy vessels, in relation to our topic.

The *Aron*'s measurements all have half-*amos*, teaching us that in regard to Torah and mitzvos, we should never feel that we have finished or completed our work. Chazal teach us that Torah is like an ocean with no end; there is always more to discover and accomplish. However, the *Shulchan*'s measurements are all complete besides for one—its height. When it comes to *parnassah*, Hashem has complete control over it, we just have to do *hishtadlus*—some basic involvement on our part.

How free we would be if we didn't feel a need to constantly check our emails, our voice mail, and our texts! If we didn't feel the pressure of responding to work-related tasks at all hours of the day and night, it would liberate us! With this mindset, with the understanding that it isn't all up to us and that only Torah should have that level of constant movement, we would surely have more *menuchas ha'nefesh*.

Concerning Torah and mitzvos, the responsibility of what we acquire is on us, as we are taught: "All has been predetermined except for our *yiras Shamayim*," i.e., our holy endeavors and the time and effort we spend on that. In those areas, there is no end.

The Kotzker Rebbe would tell his chassidim after their tefillos of the Yamim Nora'im that if they can come to him, he will let them know what they davened for and whether Hashem will be giving them what they asked for. One Yid was told that even though he davened to become wealthy so that he wouldn't have to work and have more time for learning, his request wasn't granted. The chassid asked the Kotzker Rebbe why that would be the case; doesn't Hashem want him to have all day to learn? The Rebbe said, "As you work, you are always waiting for a quiet moment between customers so that you can quickly grab your sefer and learn something. Throughout the day, you look for every opportunity to find these moments that give you such joy. Hashem loves it so much; He gets such pleasure watching your never-ending appetite for learning and how you manage to take every extra minute to glance into your sefarim! He wasn't ready to give that up."

So often do we hear people use the expression, "there is not enough time in the day," as though their excessive amount of work is the cause of their success. The Torah teaches us the total opposite. There is only one place where there is no end and limit, and that is our *avodas Hashem*—our spiritual pursuits. All else has a defined finish line.

May we merit to build a *Shulchan* that is laden with Torah and mitzvos so that it bears a striking resemblance to the Holy *Aron*, and may we measure success by our accomplishments in the world of *ruchniyus*.

Tetzaveh

THE SOUND OF SILENCE

וְאַתָּה תְּצַוֶּה אֶת בְּנֵי יִשְׂרָאֵל.

And you shall command the B'nei Yisrael.

Shemos 27:20

My Rav, Rav Moshe Weinberger of Aish Kodesh, once asked: We are accustomed to the term of וַיֹּאמֶר and וַיְדַבֵּר, so why is the term תְּצַוֶּה being used here?

He answered with the following Midrash: When Mashiach arrives, he will not need to tell Yidden what to do. People will see him, and by gazing at his face and by being in the presence of holiness, they will desire to do *teshuvah* and change their ways.

Rabbi Y.Y. Jacobson once said, "Sometimes you leave a great person and say, 'Wow, what an awesome and holy person he is!' After seeing the Lubavitcher Rebbe, people would say, 'Wow, what an awesome and holy person I am!'" By being in the mere presence of holiness, your own inner holiness is awakened.

The Torah is teaching us "*v'ata*": by being you, "*tetzaveh*"—that will "command" others what to do. Without talking or preaching, by merely doing the right thing, you will inspire those around you. We are always teachers because we have daily interactions with family, friends, and colleagues. We are always students because of these interactions as well. The greatest lessons and the strongest impressions are made from the unspoken words.

Of course, the *"va'yedaber"* and *"va'yomer"* are very often needed, as without them we would be lost and have no knowledge of what to do. But, beyond that, we should try to be *"v'ata"* people—true role models in action. There are areas of life where we have less guidance. In our offices, we don't have a *rebbi* or a spiritual counselor easily accessible. We don't have a constant *"va'yedaber"* and *"va'yomer."* In those situations, it becomes our duty to learn from the actions of the many special people around us—perhaps a boss or colleague—who, in a quiet way, make an impression. It also empowers us to becoming silent teachers just by refining ourselves.

There is a man I know who is truly a *"v'ata"* personality, one whose mere being is *"tetzaveh"* others. One day, he was having a conversation with a group of people when someone said an inappropriate joke. Immediately, though, the person apologized to my friend for using such language. My friend never told them what is right and wrong or gave them a *"shiur"* on the matter. They just knew that around him, it's *"past nisht."*

> *Rabbi Heshy Weinreb didn't consider himself a Lubavitcher. However, he lived in Crown Heights for a short time after he got married and would therefore go to the Rebbe's farbrengen from time to time. Still, his relationship with the Rebbe was always from a distance. Three years after he married, he moved to Silver Spring, Maryland, where he attended the University of Maryland. He received a PhD in psychology and began working as a psychologist in the local school system. In addition, he used to give shiurim in Gemara.*
>
> *As time went on, he had many questions. Should he stay in Torah learning, or should he continue in psychology? And if so, how should he further his career? Should he move into private psychotherapy work or accept an offer from one of the county social service organizations in the area? He also was not sure what was best for his children in terms of educational options*

in Silver Spring. He was unsure what to do or where to go. He spoke to various close friends, and one of them, a Chabad chassid, suggested that he visit the Rebbe. In February of 1971, he called the Rebbe. The Rebbe's secretary answered the phone in English with a simple "Hello, who's this?" As he was talking to the secretary, he heard the Rebbe in the background ask in Yiddish, "Who's calling?" The secretary replied, "A Yid fun Maryland—A Jew from Maryland."

He told the secretary that he had many questions that he would like to discuss with the Rebbe—questions about what direction his life should take, questions regarding his career, questions of faith, etc. He explained that he was at a very uncertain stage in his life and didn't know where to turn. He spoke in English and, as he was talking, the Rebbe's secretary was repeating and paraphrasing his words in Yiddish. Then he heard the Rebbe say in the background, in Yiddish: "Tell him that there is a Jew who lives in Maryland that he can speak to. Der Yid hayst Veinreb—his name is Weinreb."

The secretary asked him, "Did you hear what the Rebbe said?" Now, he couldn't believe his ears. He knew for sure that he had not given the secretary his name, but the Rebbe had just said his name! He was taken aback, and wanted to hear it again. So, when the secretary asked whether he heard, he said no.

The secretary repeated the Rebbe's words to him: "S'iz doh a Yid in Maryland mit vemen er zol redden. Zayn numen iz Veinreb—There's a Jew in Maryland whom he should talk to. His name is Weinreb." So he replied, "But my name is Weinreb!" And then he heard the Rebbe say, "Oib azoi, zol er visen zayn az amol darf men reden tzu zich—If that's the case, then he should know that, sometimes, one needs to speak to himself."

The secretary also seemed stunned by what was taking place, but he then said to him: "The Rebbe said that sometimes it's best to talk to yourself. Isn't your name Weinreb?"

> *"Yes, my name is Weinreb, but maybe the Rebbe means a different Weinreb."*
>
> *"No, the Rebbe's saying, 'Talk to Weinreb,' and he explained that you must to talk to yourself."*

Sometimes, by being ourselves and being true to ourselves, we can teach and inspire ourselves and others. It's not always the loud instructions that we are given that will inspire us to make a change.

Perhaps that is why Moshe Rabbeinu isn't mentioned in this *parashah*. He was taking a step back, not actively telling B'nei Yisrael what to do. There were many commands that we received from our leader, Moshe Rabbeinu. We needed them—every single one of them. That is the book of 613! Yet the lesson of *"v'ata"* is what allows all of the *"va'yedaber"*s and *"va'yomer"*'s to be properly transmitted and accepted.

May we each merit to become the "true me," the person that Hashem intended us to be when He willed our existence. And may the light that we generate shine onto others as well.

Ki Sisa

OUT OF THIS WORLD

וְהַמִּכְתָּב מִכְתַּב אֱלֹקִים הוּא
חָרוּת עַל הַלֻּחֹת.

And the inscription was God's inscription,
engraved on the tablets.

Shemos 32:16

Regarding this *pasuk*, *Pirkei Avos* says: "Do not read the word as *charus*—engraved, but rather as *cheirus*—freedom, because there is nobody as free as the one who involves himself in Torah study."[1] What does this mean, and why is it so?

Hashem looked into the Torah and created the world. Hashem and Torah were here before any other existence. Through creating the world, Hashem was able to reveal Himself. There were many stages in the process of Hashem's revelation to us, one of them being *tzimtzum*. In loose terms, the world we occupy has many layers that cover the inner *p'nimiyus*, the truest and strongest *kedushah* that comes from Hashem Himself. Any limitations we have are part of the world we live in because in Hashem's world, there are no limitations. Time and space are both concepts that we are bound to, but Hashem exists beyond

---

1 *Avos* 6:2.

both. There is, however, one way that we can pull off the shackles that we seem tied down to in this world, which is that we can transcend the natural limitations of creation by *limud Torah*, because the Holy Torah is one with Hashem. When we learn Torah, we tap into a world without limits, and the yoke of this world is taken off our shoulders. Time that did not seem available avails itself to us. Issues that were concerning us seem to dissipate. Tension and friction give way to love and connection. Torah goals that didn't seem attainable are reached beyond our wildest dreams.

Another Mishnah in *Avos* says, "Do not say, 'I will learn when I have the time,' since you may not have the time."[2] What this means is that sometimes, when glancing at our To-Do list, there really is no time. When we use "this world" eyes to approach our errands, we can't figure out how we will manage. But if we slip away to the *beis midrash* first, miraculously the list seems to shrink. Many items are taken care of, urgent matters seem less urgent. We defy the norms of this world through *limud Torah*.

This is freedom. It goes without saying that this isn't referring to a lazy person who doesn't want to work, because such a person doesn't want to learn either. As busy as we are in the office, with meetings and deadlines, pressure, and expectations, we tap into a limitless world. Whether it is before a meeting starts and we "*chap*" a Mishnah or an evening *chavrusa*, we will feel the magic of transcendence.

> *Rabbi Yisrael Gellis was cleaning out his father's drawer after he passed away, and he came upon a stack of wedding invitations. He thought it was strange that his father would have saved them. After spending a few minutes looking at them, he realized that they were all from the same year—the year his father had been in aveilus and therefore couldn't attend those specific weddings. He was amazed when he turned the invitations over, and on each one his father had written something down. It was a cheshbon of how much time he would have had*

---

2   Ibid. 2:4.

expended for that specific simchah, and he wrote: "Lekavod the new chassan and kallah, I have spent X amount of time learning Torah in their zechus." The time he spent learning matched the time he would have needed to partake in the simchah. Rabbi Gellis understood the merit of Torah learning, and furthermore, he understood the value of time. If there would have been time to go to the simchah, then there is time that can be used for learning.

May we merit knowing that what is engraved on the *Luchos* can be engraved on our hearts as well. We can live in this world and experience an out-of-world reality.

THE BIG THREE

Throughout this *parashah*, there are recurring themes that teach us that blessing comes from doing the will of Hashem. When it seems at times that by doing certain things we are losing out, the Torah is reassuring us that this will never be the case. Let's take a look at three specific examples given in this *parashah*.

In *Shemos* 34:24, the Torah tells us about the mitzvah of *aliyah la'regel*—going up to the Beis Hamikdash three times a year. One may be worried to leave his home, since thieves would have the perfect opportunity to rob an empty home, so the Torah says, "No man will desire your land when you go to be seen by Hashem your God three times a year."

We can take this promise of safety a step further. The Torah is saying that the actual leaving of your house will protect it from robbers. Alarms and triple-lock systems are not the ultimate protection! Hashem says that when you leave your home to go to His home, that act of leaving it will guard it!

Second, in *Shemos* 34:1, Hashem tells Moshe Rabbeinu to carve the second set of tablets with the words: "Carve for yourself." Chazal (brought in *Rashi*) say that Hashem was telling Moshe Rabbeinu that the carvings, i.e., the bits of stone that were carved out, are for him. Moshe Rabbeinu became wealthy from this as they were made from Sanpiron—a sapphire stone that was extremely valuable. The Geonim tell us that the entire Torah is found within the *Aseres Hadibros*, so essentially they represent all of Torah. Moshe Rabbbeinu's wealth came directly from the Torah; ours does as well.

Third, concerning the *machatzis ha'shekel*, the half-shekel coin, the Torah says, "The wealthy should not give more, and the poor should not decrease from the half-*shekel*."[1] When it came to the mitzvah of giving the half-*shekel*, more or less wasn't good. Hashem wanted exactly only a half-*shekel* from each person. A generous person may have desired to give more, but he couldn't because Hashem wanted a half and no more. One would think that if all the coins were a donation to the Beis Hamikdash and benefiting the *hekdesh* account, it would be a mitzvah to give more. This wasn't the case. The greatest donation one can give to Hashem is fulfilling His will.

Many years ago in America, it was very difficult for a Jew to hold down a job. When it would come to Friday and the Jew said he couldn't come in on Shabbos, he would be told, "then don't bother showing up on Sunday!" There is a story told of a Jew who experienced this, and over time he received many pink slips, reminding him of his commitment to Shabbos and the price he was paying to keep Shabbos. Every time he received a pink slip, he would take the pink slip, kiss it, and put it away in a box under his bed.

When Sukkos came, he managed to find some old boards and doors and put together a Sukkah. Then he took the box from under his bed and covered the walls of the sukkah with his precious pink slips. He then called his children down into the sukkah and he showed them his decorations. As he pointed to one slip, he said, "This is one Shabbos that we kept." Then he pointed to another one and said, "This is another Shabbos that we kept."

Instead of dwelling on his difficult situation and tribulation, he took every single one of those pink slips and turned them into a sukkah decoration. That was his beautification of his sukkah, and there was nothing more pleasing in the eyes of Hashem.

---

1   *Shemos* 30:15.

May we all merit to constantly remember the true source of all wealth. Although at times, we may think that doing a specific action will bring profit, the greatest "prophet" teaches us that a connection to the *Luchos* and all they represent will bring us true wealth.

Vayakhel

IT'S OFF TO WORK WE GO

שֵׁשֶׁת יָמִים תֵּעָשֶׂה מְלָאכָה וּבַיּוֹם
הַשְּׁבִיעִי יִהְיֶה לָכֶם קֹדֶשׁ שַׁבַּת
שַׁבָּתוֹן לַה׳.

Six days work may be done, but on the
seventh day you shall have sanctity,
a day of complete rest for Hashem.
Shemos 35:2

Rav Shlomo Ganzfried, author of the *Kitzur Shulchan Aruch*,
asks: Why is it necessary that the Torah commands us to work
for six days and then Shabbos will be holy? Why not simply skip the
first part and tell us right away that Shabbos is a special day?

He answers that the Torah is teaching us how truly special Shabbos
really is. One may think that "they" work all week, but on Shabbos they
take a break. Look closer at the *pasuk*. The word תֵּעָשֶׂה means "it shall be
done." The grammatical usage is teaching us that we are not really the
ones doing the work. Instead, it happens, as if on its own. If we fully
comprehend that even during the work week, it is Hashem doing it,
then "the seventh day will (truly) be holy."

The rest we experience on Shabbos is the belief that it is all from
Hashem. The greater the recognition of this, the greater the holiness

85

we will experience on Shabbos. It will not be interest rates that will "interest" us at our Shabbos table discussion. Instead of talking about rent control, we will remember Who is in control of our rent!

Who takes pride in how nicely they breathe? Nobody would, as it is obvious that they aren't responsible for their gift of breathing. Neither would one take pride in the creation of the world, as they have no involvement in that either. This helps us distance ourselves from *gaavah*. We don't show off what is clearly not the product of our own doing. All week, we either can get caught up in our productivity, or we can focus on remembering that the week is תֵּעָשֶׂה. Yes, we do our part, but it's happening by the greatest power of all.

> *In August 1939, Rav Yaakov Yosef Herman decided that he and his wife would live the rest of their lives in the holiness of Eretz Yisrael. After a few months of packing, they set sail on their voyage. The original schedule called for their ship to dock at Haifa port on a Wednesday, and after a few days in Haifa, they would journey to Yerushalayim where they would live. After the captain was warned about possibly mined waters due to the outbreak of WWII, the boat was detoured to a safer route, only to dock a few days late with only an hour before sunset on Friday afternoon.*
>
> *The loudspeakers on the boat ordered the passengers to disembark immediately and claim their baggage at once. It was clear that if the Hermans stuck around to claim any of their belongings, they would not make it anywhere before Shabbos. Rav Herman asked to speak with the head customs officer. The man listened as Rav Herman explained, "I have never desecrated the Sabbath in my life. To arrive here in the Holy Land and desecrate it is impossible." Tears rolled down Rav Herman's face.*
>
> *The officer curtly replied, "Rabbi, there is nothing I can do."*
>
> *"Just stamp our passports and let us through. We'll pick up our baggage after the Sabbath," pleaded Rav Herman.*

The officer then explained, "That would be impossible. We are removing all the baggage from the ship and leaving it on the pier. Once the boat clears port, everything must be cleared off it also."

"I don't care about the luggage", replied Rav Herman, "please just stamp our passports so we can leave."

The officer looked at Rav Herman inquiringly and asked, "How much baggage do you have?" "Sixteen crates in the hold, and nine suitcases in our cabin," came the reply.

"Do you realize," the officer added, "that once you leave, your baggage will be on the pier with no one responsible for it? By tomorrow night you will not find any of your belongings. The Arabs will have stolen them all!"

"I have no alternative," Rav Herman explained. "It's almost time for the Sabbath. We must get to the city in time. Please, please, just clear our passports and let us go."

The officer, astounded, called to another officer, "Stamp their passports and let them through. This rabbi is willing to lose all his belongings in order to get into the city in time for their Sabbath."

As soon as the Hermans were off the boat, they jumped into a taxi that rushed them to their Shabbos destination. They arrived just in time for Mrs. Herman to light Shabbos candles.

May we merit weeks of work infused with holiness so that our Shabbos experience will truly be *kodesh*!

Pekudei

YOUR FINGERPRINTS

כְּכֹל אֲשֶׁר צִוָּה ה׳ אֶת מֹשֶׁה כֵּן עָשׂוּ
בְּנֵי יִשְׂרָאֵל אֵת כָּל הָעֲבֹדָה. וַיַּרְא
מֹשֶׁה אֶת כָּל הַמְּלָאכָה וְהִנֵּה עָשׂוּ
אֹתָהּ כַּאֲשֶׁר צִוָּה ה׳ כֵּן עָשׂוּ וַיְבָרֶךְ
אֹתָם מֹשֶׁה.

In accordance with all that Hashem had
commanded Moshe, so did the children of
Israel do all the work. Moshe saw the entire
work, and behold! They had done it; as
Hashem had commanded, so had they done,
and Moshe blessed them.

Shemos 39:42–43

Couldn't these two *pesukim* have been easily combined into one
pasuk and simply state that they did the work and Moshe gave
them a *berachah*? What can be taught from these two *pesukim*?

Rabbi Moshe Weinberger quotes Rav Soloveitchik, who explains
that the difference between these two *pesukim* is that the first *pasuk* is
speaking about *avodah*, while the second is speaking of *melachah*. These
are two different words with two different implications. *Avodah* is the

act of doing a specific job but remaining distant from it. One can do the job perfectly yet forge no connection with it. *Melachah*, on the other hand, is doing the job and connecting with it. Not only is the work being done, but a personal imprint is left on the handiwork.

An artist does not usually finish his masterpiece and walk away; he will most likely sign his name at the bottom. He takes pride in his work and sees himself in what he created. In other jobs, it very often depends on the person. Some will put their heart and soul into the work, while others will complete the task at hand with no personal connection to what was done.

In *pasuk* 42, the *avodah* was done, the task was completed, but it didn't reflect those who were involved in it. In *pasuk* 43, it says, "Moshe saw." There was something special to see; it was the personal touch—the way B'nei Yisrael connected with the commandment that they were given. The pride that they had in doing the will of Hashem was evident in the finished product. When Moshe Rabbeinu saw this, the *pasuk* says, "He blessed them!"

Rashi says that the *berachah* he gave them was that "the presence of Hashem should rest in the work of their hands," i.e., that all the work that they do should have the fingerprints of Hashem, the stamp of Hashem, and that the work should glorify His Name.

This message can be applied in a very practical way. There is so much "*avodah*" that we are all involved in—both mundane and holy. Where do we take the *avodah* to the level of *melachah*? From all the tasks that we have, which are those that we take spiritual pride in, and in doing connect to Hashem? And even further, within what seems like mundane *avodah*, we can choose to leave spiritual fingerprints. How we conduct ourselves in the workplace and how we use our speech is up to us. Just as we sanctify our food with a *berachah rishonah* and *acharonah*, and just as we begin our day with *Modeh Ani* and end with *Shema*, the choice is ours. We can stamp the logo of Hashem on all that we do.

> *Meir, a construction company owner in Brooklyn, passed away before his time, and yet there are reminders of him all over town as his handiwork and craftsmanship are enjoyed daily.*

Over the years, he would drive to construction sights, and his heart would be pained as he saw so many elderly people standing and waiting for city buses, as the small benches were already occupied. He lovingly built many benches and placed them at those crowded areas, and rejoiced when he saw the elderly sitting comfortably when he drove past. This was a man whose heart and soul left a deep and lasting imprint on all he created.

May we merit taking all of our *avodah* to the level of *melachah*, and then we will see the *berachah* of Moshe, "שֶׁתִּשְׁרֶה שְׁכִינָה," that Hashem's presence should be in our lives as well.

HEAVY LIFTING

וַיְהִי בַּחֹדֶשׁ הָרִאשׁוֹן בַּשָּׁנָה הַשֵּׁנִית
בְּאֶחָד לַחֹדֶשׁ הוּקַם הַמִּשְׁכָּן.

*It came to pass in the first month, in the
second year, on the first day of the month,
that the Mishkan was set up.*

Shemos 40:17

When discussing the actual building of the *Mishkan*, the pasuk says that it was "set up," using a passive term. *Rashi*, in an earlier *pasuk*, explains that Moshe Rabbeinu realized how heavy the beams were, and so he asked Hashem, "How can anyone put these up?" Hashem answered, "Make it look like you are lifting them, do your part, and it will end up standing on its own." That is why the *pasuk* says, "it was put up." Even though Moshe Rabbeinu did try to lift it, it was miraculously erected by Hashem.

We learn the importance of doing our part, even when a task seems daunting and seemingly impossible. Hashem gives us our power, and we can't lift a finger without Him. But by lifting, i.e., doing our responsibility, we accept that He wants us to invest basic energy and capabilities.

The Gemara in *Arachin* says that when a firstborn animal is born, it has an automatic status of *kedushah*. Without anyone sanctifying it,

91

it is *kadosh*. Why then, do the Chachamim say that we should verbally *mekadesh* it? It is already born with holiness!

Hashem wants us to contribute and be an active part of the *kedushah*. It is a mitzvah when we verbally state the *kedushah* of the animal; it is our active involvement. The same goes with all mitzvos and all areas of our life. While we understand that Hashem will "erect the *Mishkan*," He gives us opportunities to be part of the process, always acknowledging that it can't be done with our strength alone.

When we realize that it is truly all Hashem and not us, then so much pressure is lifted off of our backs. We must do our part, but ultimately it is all Him.

Mr. Cohen was having a hard time finding a job that would allow him to keep Shabbos. He had recently arrived in America and was adamant about shemiras Shabbos. Finally, he found a job offer to be a shamash—a caretaker in a shul. He was very close to having the job, but he had to meet with the shul board to make it official. At the meeting, one of the board members asked him if he spoke English. "We have people who rent the shul facility, which requires that the shamash be able to converse with them," he said. Mr. Cohen answered that he did not know English, and the interview came to an abrupt end.

Without any job, Mr. Cohen decided to get a pushcart to try to sell odds and ends on the street. Surprisingly, it went well. He got another cart and hired a young man to sell his wares. He continued to expand his business until it turned into a store and eventually to a few stores. He became a success.

Business kept growing, and at one point he was investing in a large deal. At the meeting, the other company owner handed him a contract. Without looking at it, he handed it to his secretary, who read it to him. "You can't read English?" the fellow asked him in shock.

"If I could read English," Mr. Cohen responded, "I would still be cleaning shuls."

We do our part, and Hashem does His!

May we merit lifting the vessels of our life and feeling the lightness that comes when we know that the weight of the world does not sit on our shoulders.

Sefer Vayikra

Vayikra

SACRIFICE AT WORK

אָדָם כִּי יַקְרִיב מִכֶּם קָרְבָּן.

*When a man from [among] you
brings a sacrifice.*

Vayikra 1:2

The concept of *korbanos* is beyond us, but there are many lessons and insights to be gleaned from this lofty *avodah*.

A *Korban Shelamim* is mostly enjoyed by the owner, unlike a *Korban Olah*, which, aside from the hide, goes completely to Hashem, and a *Korban Chatas*, which is divided between Hashem and the Kohanim. While other types of *korbanos* are accepted from the other nations, a *Korban Shelamim* can only be brought by a Jew. Why?

Only a Yid is capable of seeing pure *kedushah* within a *davar chomri*—something materialistic. Only one who believes *b'emunah sheleimah* in creation can see Hashem in even an animal. However, those who see creation as a non-Godly entity divide the world into two separate categories—physical and spiritual.

When Rabbi Shimon Bar Yochai emerged from the cave and saw people involved in mundane pursuits, his eyes burned them. Hashem then said to him, "Return to your cave. The world I created has *melachah*—seemingly mundane activity." The second time he came out, he saw a man running. It was *bein ha'shemashos*, right before Shabbos, a time that is between day and night, which combines the elements of *kodesh* and *chol*. This was a clear sign to him that the world contains both elements—mundane and holiness.

The Mishnah in *Avos* says, "He who walks along a road, studying, and interrupts his studies to say, 'How beautiful is this tree, how beautiful is this field!' the Torah considers it as though he transgressed against his own soul."[1]

Why is that so bad? Aren't the trees and fields all part of His wondrous creations?

The answer lies in one word of the Mishnah: "he interrupts." This person sees the world as semi-detached from the *sefarim* he learns, partially disconnected from *kedushah*. He sees it as an interruption to his Torah study. That is where he is wrong.

Let's return to our *pasuk*. When we bring a *korban*, remember "מִכֶּם"—remember **you**, the Yid bringing the *korban*! Although we are material people, we are infused with a holy *neshamah*. So too, our *korbanos*, our animals, and whatever other physicality we are connected to, also has a true, inner essence that we are meant to reveal.

Our workday feels so mundane, lacking in holiness. Yet, we can remember that through our *avodah*, we can bring an elevated *korban*.

My son-in-law, Shlomo Karmely, showed me a beautiful *vort* from the *Meleches Shlomo*. The Beis Hamikdash was filled with the holiest work. Everyone wanted the merit to be able to do some *avodah* there. In fact, we daven for its return every day! But what took place there? Shiurim or learning? No, it was the *avodah* and service that Hashem told them to do. It was slaughtering animals, sprinkling blood, flour offerings, and wine and oil libations. What seems to be mundane was the holiest of the holies! Why? Because they were fulfilling the will of Hashem.

May we merit bringing a *Korban Shelamim*—enjoying the discovery of the inherent holiness within what seems the lowliest of tasks and activities—and through our efforts may we ultimately be bringing it in the Beis Hamikdash.

---

1   *Avos* 3:7.

Tzav

A SPOONFUL OF UNDERSTANDING

צַו אֶת אַהֲרֹן וְאֶת בָּנָיו לֵאמֹר.

Command Aharon and his sons, saying.

Vayikra 6:2

Rashi on this verse quotes a *Toras Kohanim*: Rav Shimon says that whenever a loss of money is involved, the term *"Tzav,"* which is a strong commanding term, is used. The *Ramban* challenges *Rashi* by asking where the loss of money is with the commandment of *Korban Olah*. The Yisrael brings it; there is no cost to the Kohen. As a matter of fact, the Kohen gets the hide from it, so he actually gains! True, the Kohen gets less than other *korbanos*, but one can't say that they're losing.

The *Gur Aryeh* explains *Rashi* in the following way: True, the Kohen didn't lose from the *korban* itself, but in the time he was bringing the *korban*, he could have been at work, making "real" money. Instead, he is leaving work and coming to bring the *korban* and only receiving the skin of the animal. This is why it is considered a monetary loss.

There is a special lesson to be learned here. The Kohanim are a very small and elite group. They have the exclusive rights of working in the house of Hashem, and they have access to parts of the Beis Hamikdash

99

that nobody else can enter. If anyone would overstep their boundaries and try to do the Kohanim's job, they are potentially deserving of severe punishment. All firstborn animals go to the Kohen, as well as all the first fruits. The Kohen gets *terumah*, the first tithe of the crops, and a portion of the dough also goes to them. What about the *korbanos*? They receive a nice portion from most *korbanos*. They, and not the owner, receive a part from the *Korban Chatas* and *Korban Asham*. Is it, then, really such a loss if they only receive the hides from this *Korban Olah*? The Kohen doesn't even pay for the animal. Is the Torah really concerned with the losses that may be incurred from not working?

Yes. The Torah understands human nature, and it understands that it is natural for someone to be concerned when they could possibly be making more, or doing more, at the present moment. There is tremendous *chizuk* to be gained with this knowledge. Hashem is with us while we make our *parnassah*, and he understands our struggles and our humanity.

In the early 1900s, there was a young boy standing on a lunch line at Yeshivas Eitz Chaim in Yerushalayim. He was so excited, because a special delicacy was being given to the boys that day—chocolate pudding. He ran back on the line to receive another portion, although he knew that it was one per child. The cook got upset at him, as some of the boys did not even get once yet, and he yelled at him in front of everybody. The boy got so embarrassed and upset that he knocked over the tray of puddings. They all ended up in a chocolate mess on the floor!

He got yelled at and was told that he must go see Rav Aryeh Levin, the Mashgiach, the following day. As you can imagine, he was filled with anxiety and trepidation as he made his way to the small office of Rav Aryeh. He assumed he would be severely punished and probably kicked out of the yeshiva for what he had done. He sat across from the tzaddik, and Rav Aryeh smiled and asked him: "Do you regret what you did, and are you sorry about it?"

"Of course, I feel terrible," responded the young boy.

"I'm happy to hear that. Please don't do that again," said Rav Aryeh. He then proceeded to remove two small chocolate puddings from his desk. "Here, let's enjoy these puddings together, as chocolate pudding is one of my favorite treats as well."

In his brilliant way, Rav Aryeh educated the boy and made sure to let him know that he understood exactly what he had been going through. The young boy never forgot the spoonful of love he received with the spoonful of pudding on that day.

May we all be *zocheh* to realize the love and understanding Hashem has for us. The more we feel it, the more we will reciprocate it.

Shemini

LIGHT A SIMPLE FIRE

וַתֵּצֵא אֵשׁ מִלִּפְנֵי ה' וַתֹּאכַל עַל
הַמִּזְבֵּחַ אֶת הָעֹלָה וְאֶת הַחֲלָבִים
וַיַּרְא כָּל הָעָם וַיָּרֹנּוּ וַיִּפְּלוּ עַל פְּנֵיהֶם.

*And fire went forth from before Hashem and
consumed the burnt offering and the fats
upon the Altar, and all the people saw, sang
praises, and fell upon their faces.*

Vayikra 9:24

This wonderous phenomenon, a fire coming down from shamayim, was a constant miracle on the *Mizbei'ach*. Chazal teach us that "even though a fire comes down from *shamayim*, there is still a mitzvah to bring it מִן הַהֶדְיוֹט—from you."

Why do Chazal use the term הֶדְיוֹט, implying simplicity and lack of greatness? It seems that the main point is that a heavenly fire isn't enough; a "person" also needs to light the fire. So why not say "from man"?

We all know that Hashem runs the world from the simplest acts to the greatest miracles. It's all from Him. We do our *hishtadlus*, what is required of us both in mitzvos and wordly matters, but ultimately, we know that it is all Him. The more we focus on this knowledge, the more humbled we feel. Haughtiness falls away as we recognize *gadlus ha'Borei*.

Just as we are naturally humbled when we find ourselves in the presence of greatness, even more so when we feel the presence of Hashem.

Rabbi Dovid Trenk, *zt"l*, was an outstanding and charismatic educator with a tall presence and an overflowing personality. However, when he stood in front of *tzaddikim*, he became so quiet, meek, and small. He seemed to shrink in their presence, and people that saw him were surprised that he was the same Rabbi Trenk that danced on tables at weddings.

The word הֶדְיוֹט means simple, completely empty of haughtiness. Chazal are teaching us that even though fire comes from Heaven, and all that happens is brought down by Hashem, it is up to us to bring our own fire. We must do our part, our *chelek*, in the service of Hashem. But what should we remember as we do our part? מִן הַהֶדְיוֹט—it should be with the total realization that I am nothing on my own, and מִלְּפְנֵי ה'—it's always before Hashem. When we remember this, we will always remain "simple" and humble before our Creator.

Later in the *parashah*, we have the story of Nadav and Avihu. The *pasuk* says that "וַתֵּצֵא אֵשׁ מִלְּפְנֵי ה' וַתֹּאכַל אוֹתָם—A fire came forth from before Hashem and consumed them."[1] There are different opinions as to what their sin was that prompted their death. One common denominator among the explanations, though, is that what they did wasn't the *ratzon Hashem*. They brought a fire that Hashem never told them to bring. Twice, the *pasuk* says מִלְּפְנֵי ה'—a fire came from "before Hashem," and they died "before Hashem."

When we recognize that we are in the presence of Hashem, our own ideas and thoughts take a backseat to what Hashem wants of us. When they were punished for bringing "their own fire," the Torah stresses the origin of the fire—from "before Hashem." The Torah then says that they died "before Hashem." The *pesukim* are showing us a very clear picture of where they went wrong.

As we go about our day, no matter where we are, or whom we are with, we are before Hashem. This gives us constant direction about how

---

1   *Vayikra* 10:2.

to conduct ourselves. Furthermore, we are never alone. Even when it seems so void of *kedushah*, He is there with us.

May we always feel that we are in the presence of Hashem and act accordingly. May we be *zocheh* to bring a fire of humility.

Tazria-Metzora

A PARENT'S LOVE

From the unique and severe punishments of *lashon hara*, to the amount of positive and negative commandments that the Chafetz Chaim calculates, it is clear that *lashon hara* is severely disliked by Hashem. What it so unique about this *aveirah* that it has so many consequences?

My Rav, Rav Moshe Weinberger, says the following: If, God forbid, you were to overhear someone speak negatively about your child, how would you feel? Even if we were sharing something that bothered us about our child with someone else and the other person agreed, it would upset us and hurt deeply. When someone says something nice and praises our child, we love the person for what they said.

Rabbi Weinberger had a friend who always told Rabbi Weinberger's mother how great he is. This friend did nothing more than praise his friend to his mother, and Mrs. Weinberger loved him! He was on the top of her list—all because he spoke well of her son. In fact, she always managed to give that friend the biggest piece of cake.

We are all the children of a very loving parent—*Hakadosh Baruch Hu*. He loves us with the greatest love ever! We all have a *chelek* of Hashem within us; it doesn't get much closer than that. Now imagine that Hashem hears someone speak badly about one of His children. How does He feel? The pain is too great to bear! He loves us more than a parent loves a child. What *nachas* it is for Hashem when He hears one Jew speak nicely about another Jew! Is there any greater feeling than when you see your children taking care of each other?

Is it such a shock to us, then, that *lashon hara* gets so much negative attention in the Torah? Is it a wonder why the punishment is so severe?

The Arizal teaches us that it is very important to begin our day with the mitzvah of "Love your friend as you love yourself." As we begin our day and ask Him for success, the greatest way to "get on His good side" is to take care of His children.

There was once a Yid who went to complain to a *tzaddik* that someone opened up a business just like his, right across the street from him! The *tzaddik* responded, "You want *hatzlachah*? Daven for the other Yid that he should do well. Have him in mind in your *tefillos*."

How appropriate would it be if that is how we felt and dealt with our competitors!

The best investment advice is that you should help another Yid if you want Hashem to help you.

Reb Itzele of Volozhin writes in the introduction of his father's *sefer*, *Nefesh Hachaim*, that his father always said, "The purpose of a person in this world is to help others with all the strength that he has."

May we all be *zocheh* to give our Father in Heaven *nachas* from our actions and interactions with His other children. The more we focus on the greatness of a Yid and not his faults, we will see him in a positive light. Our speech will follow our thoughts, and Hashem will have *nachas* from all of us.

LIKE A CHICKEN WITHOUT A HEAD

Do we ever feel as if we are running after our *parnassah* like a chicken without a head? Do we get overwhelmed at times? What can we keep in mind that will help us during these moments?

There is a beautiful Midrash that I saw in the *sefer Shabbos Vort*:

> *There was a poor Kohen who thought that if he would leave Eretz Yisrael, perhaps he could find a better livelihood. Before he left, he went to discuss his plan with his wife. He felt bad that he was leaving the community without a Kohen to check their potential tzaraas. He decided to teach her how to examine the marks so she can take his place when he left. She agreed, and he began to teach her the halachos.*
>
> *"It is important to know that when you observe the hair," he said, "each strand grows from a separate opening, and each one is nourished from its own follicle. If you see that the opening around the hair has dried out, the person has tzaraas."*
>
> *She listened and responded, "Listen to your own words. If Hashem has provided each hair on the body with a wellspring from which it draws its sustenance, how much more so you—His very handiwork! Why must you wander to chutz la'aretz in search of parnassah?"*
>
> *The Kohen listened and didn't leave Eretz Yisrael.*

If we remember the Source of our *parnassah*, the signer of our checks, it would allow us to redirect a lot of our strength. "God has many messengers." Hashem has many ways to help us with our livelihood. If our priorities are correct, and we emphasize the eternal—the service of Hashem and the *chinuch* of our children—we have done our part. What we end up receiving is up to Him, and just as Hashem is nourishing each hair on our head, He takes care of our *parnassah* as well. We don't need to worry that someone else is taking our clients or customers—He has your back!

Tzaraas is called a נֶגַע—an affliction, but when read backwards it is עֹנֶג—a pleasure. Sometimes what looks like it will be bad for *parnassah* can actually be the source of our success.

There is a Yid I know, Reb Reuven Wolf. A major corporation leased property from him, and the agreement stipulated was that after a certain number of years, he would start collecting an increase of ten percent. However, after some time he realized that they had started paying him the increase two years early. Without delay, he called the leasee and informed them of the substantial overpayment.

When we know that Hashem is giving us our blessing, we have a much easier time being honest. If it's not ours, it's not ours.

May we merit strengthening ourselves with this knowledge so that if we ever find ourselves worrying about *parnassah*, we will overcome with *emunah*.

Acharei Mos

FALLING OFF THE DEEP END

וְהַשָּׂעִיר אֲשֶׁר עָלָה עָלָיו הַגּוֹרָל
לַעֲזָאזֵל יָעֳמַד חַי לִפְנֵי ה' לְכַפֵּר עָלָיו
לְשַׁלַּח אֹתוֹ לַעֲזָאזֵל הַמִּדְבָּרָה.

And the he-goat upon which the lot "for Azazel" came up, shall be placed while still alive, before Hashem, to [initiate] atonement upon it, and to send it away to Azazel, into the desert.

Vayikra 16:10

The topic of the *Azazel* is difficult to understand, and yet there are different lessons and reasons that are given that allow us to grow through this *chok*.

The goat, which is called a שָׂעִיר, is a reference to Eisav, who settled in the land of שֵׂעִיר. We know that Eisav chose the path and portion of material pursuits. We throw it off the cliff, representing our desire to cast off our pursuits of *gashmiyus* and the ways of Eisav. We still go to work the day after Yom Kippur, but we do so to accomplish not just in this world but in the next. We are physically here, but we are accomplishing there.

In addition, we cast off all unnecessary work—the over-exertion. There is a heavy yoke that we carry when we think it is all up to us, thinking, "The more I do, the more I have." We throw away the mindset of Eisav and accept the path of Yaakov: אִישׁ תָּם, complete and wholesome, יֹשֵׁב אֹהָלִים, a tent dweller. He saw the purpose of this world and understood that it is a means to the Next World. Houses can confuse us and make us think that there is ultimate purpose in the house. A tent, by contrast, is simple; it is clear that a tent is only there to allow one to have a safe place to live, to do, and to accomplish.

> *The Gemara in Kesubos (8b) says that Rav Chiya bar Abba would teach the children of Reish Lakish. For three days, he didn't show up. When he finally returned, Reish Lakish asked him why he hadn't come, and he said, "My father left me hanging vines of grapes, and I was harvesting them. The first day, I picked three hundred grapes, and each cluster produced a se'ah of wine. The second day, I picked three hundred more grapes, and every two clusters produced a se'ah of wine. The third day, I also picked three hundred grapes, and it took three clusters to produce a se'ah of wine. There was so much left over that I abandoned more than half."*
>
> *Reish Lakish responded, "If you had not been absent from learning, it would have produced even more." Each day that he was away from teaching, the wine production decreased. The Maharsha points out that had he stayed with his talmidim, Hashem would have gotten others to harvest for him.*

Working more is not always more. If a *navi* would tell you that a certain stock will drop continuously, would you still invest in it? It would be so clear to you that you are wasting your money. Investing in a way that is not aligned with the Torah is not wise; it will be a waste of time and money.

May we merit to cast away the endless pursuits of materialism and the notion that we are in control. Then, all we will be left with is the other שָׂעִיר—the one that is for Hashem.

Kedoshim

TILL DEATH DO US PART

דַּבֵּר אֶל כָּל עֲדַת בְּנֵי יִשְׂרָאֵל
וְאָמַרְתָּ אֲלֵהֶם קְדֹשִׁים תִּהְיוּ.

Speak to the entire congregation
of the children of Israel, and say to them,
"You shall be holy."

Vayikra 19:2

How does one make himself holy? How can we act to fulfill this mitzvah?

The Gemara tells us that when one gets married, he consecrates his wife in a way similar to that of *hekdesh*.[1] Typically, this term is used for something that is sanctified for the Beis Hamikdash. By declaring it as such, nobody else is allowed to benefit from it. One who benefits from it commits the sin of *me'ilah*—desecration of a sanctified item. So too, when one is married, upon the completion of the *kiddushin*, the woman is now designated and connected to one person only, i.e., her husband. What was available to her before is no longer available.

Rashi says "*kedushah*" is a term of separation. Hence, the term "*kiddushin*" by marriage and the name of the tractate that deals with it.

---

1   *Kiddushin* 2a.

The mitzvah of our *parashah*—to be holy—is to live life with the clarification of to Whom I am really connected; to Whom I give the ultimate *kavod*; to Whom I give the greatest thanks; and to Whom I wish to fulfill their every desire.

In fact, we know that Klal Yisrael is like a *kallah*, and the Torah and Hashem are the *chassan*. The *pasuk* says, וְאָמַרְתָּ אֲלֵהֶם. The word אֲלֵהֶם is an acronym for the famous words said at every wedding: "הֲרֵי אַתְּ מְקֻדֶּשֶׁת לִי—Behold, you are sanctified to me." It is these words that seal the bond of husband and wife—the bond of loyalty. "You are mine"—to the exclusion of all others. This is the mitzvah we have toward Hashem. We are His, we serve Him and no one else. We bow to Him and no one else.

There is a large real-estate client that I am fortunate to do business with. Even when he is involved in a large deal, where disturbances are not welcome, everything stops when he gets a phone call from his wife!

There is so much pulling us in other directions. The desire for wealth and honor are all enticements of this world. But just as a husband and wife have such recognition, so too, He is the only One for us.

There is a saying that people are "married" to their jobs. We must know who we are really married to.

Once we fulfill this, the *pasuk* says, "You are holy!"

May we be *zocheh* to fulfill this mitvah to the best of our ability, and in that merit, "בַּיּוֹם הַהוּא יִהְיֶה ה' אֶחָד וּשְׁמוֹ אֶחָד," once He is known to all as *Echad*, the only One, we will be *zocheh* to the time of Mashiach!

Emor

REAP YOUR REWARDS

לֶעָנִי וְלַגֵּר תַּעֲזֹב אֹתָם
אֲנִי ה׳ אֱלֹקֵיכֶם.

You shall leave these for the poor person and
for the stranger. I am Hashem your God.
Vayikra 23:22

Although the *parashah* deals primarily with the Kohanim and Yomim Tovim, it also briefly discusses *pe'ah*—leaving parts of the field harvest to the poor.

Rashi quotes a Mishnah in *masechta Pe'ah* and the *Toras Kohanim* that say that the Torah stresses leaving it so that the poor could gather it, essentially saying that the owner should not help them. Why is this the case? Why can't we do a little bit more *chessed* and help them collect it?

Rabbi Yissachar Frand says that an important lesson is being taught here. If we were to help them pick it up and lift it with our own hands, we would feel like it is ours. We would feel like the *baal ha'bayis*—that we are doing them a great service by giving them our goods. We may think, "It's mine, and I am gracious enough to give it to you." Therefore, the Torah instructs us not to help them because it's not ours; it belongs to the poor man. Hashem has just given us the opportunity to deliver the goods.

This is a lesson to all of us with regard to all forms of charity. Our money is from Hashem, and He gave it to us so that we can give to another. If we view it in this way, it is much easier to give tzedakah.

We can take this a step further and understand that when the opportunity to give tzedakah comes our way, it is Hashem giving us a gift on a golden platter. The greatest beneficiary of this transaction is us, the giver, not the poor man who seems to be receiving. He will get his money regardless; if Hashem wants him to have it, there are many ways for Him to send it. However, it is for us the giver to merit a chance to be the one to give. Bearing this in mind, it is not just easier to give, but rather we also understand how lucky we are.

Unfortunately, many times, collectors are told to "come to my office tomorrow." They then schlep to the city to wait in with the secretary so that the very "*chashuv* businessman" can give him a check. He could have been given it yesterday at his home or by his shul!

My friend recalled that when he grew up, if a *meshulach* were to come to his home, his father would give him the greatest honor. He would seat him at his dining-room table and make sure he was given something to eat and drink. It was clear that they were the lucky ones. Sadly, in many homes these people are ignored or turned away. We are turning away a gift from Hashem by turning away the *meshulach*. We feel like the generous *baal ha'bayis* because we believe it is our money, but if we understand that it's really not our money and it's not our home, we can open up our hands to give and be grateful for the opportunity.

Earlier in the *perek*, the *parashah* speaks about the *Korban Omer* brought on Pesach. An *omer* is a measurement equal to one-tenth of an *eiphah*. Why is that the name of the *korban*? Because this *korban* is brought at the start of the new harvest, a time when we can feel like "it's all mine, look how well I did!" So along comes the *omer*, the same measurement of the *mann* that we received everyday in the *midbar*, as the Torah says, "an *omer* per person." There was no mistake identifying exactly Who provided the *mann* and where the Source was. It was so clear that it was Hashem; nobody thought that they had a hand in the *mann* preparation. Hashem is telling us to treat the *omer* of Pesach the same way. Before we take smug pride in our harvest, remember that it is an *omer* as well.

May we merit to be givers that truly understand the gift of giving, and may all that we harvest fill us with thanks to Hashem and a desire to share.

Behar

HONEST TO GOODNESS

וְכִי תִמְכְּרוּ מִמְכָּר לַעֲמִיתֶךָ אוֹ קָנֹה
מִיַּד עֲמִיתֶךָ אַל תּוֹנוּ אִישׁ אֶת אָחִיו.

And when you make a sale to your fellow
Jew or make a purchase from the hand
of your fellow Jew, you shall not wrong
one another.

Vayikra 25:14

This *pasuk* comes in the middle of the *pesukim* that deal with *shemittah*. The simple connection is as *Rashi* explains: Since every sale of land ends with *yovel*, make sure that you charge appropriately, meaning that if there are many years left until *yovel*, the price should be higher, and if there are only a few years left, the price should be lower.

I thought of another connection between these two topics as well. The Torah is helping us attain true and total honesty. We might never consider outright theft, yet we sometimes find loopholes for financial gain. These loopholes are not 100 percent kosher, yet we allow ourselves leniency. We may use language that is not an outright lie, yet it isn't 100 percent true either. So, the Torah is telling us to learn from *shemittah*. Nobody is working, and yet everyone has what they need. In fact, there is even more *berachah* in a *shemittah* year!

Our success doesn't come from our clever tactics; it comes from Hashem. He told us not to work the land, and therefore, we don't. If we take this lesson to heart, we will see no purpose in being slightly deceitful or conniving in our business. It won't help us in the long run. Furthermore, the more honest we are, the more Hashem will give us.

We know that Chazal teach us that "falsehood has no legs." Nothing can hold it up because ultimately Hashem supports everything, and if He doesn't hold it up, it collapses. The stamp of Hashem is *emes*—truth, so by taking a path of *sheker*—deceit, we lose God's support. And He isn't a partner you want to lose!

> *A friend of mine was once in the process of closing a deal where he was purchasing a large property. As he was reading through the fine print, it looked as though he had been undercharged 2.3 million dollars. He let the owners know, and they were quite surprised at his honesty. They would have never likely realized the mistake!*
>
> *Toward the end of the proceedings, it became apparent that the property location was in a different tax zone then they had originally perceived. The new price after the adjustments was—you guessed it—approximately 2.3 million dollars less!*

May we merit taking the honest route in all that we do and have the stamp of approval of our greatest supporter, i.e., Hashem Himself.

A BINDING CONTRACT

כִּי לִי בְנֵי יִשְׂרָאֵל עֲבָדִים עֲבָדַי הֵם
אֲשֶׁר הוֹצֵאתִי אוֹתָם מֵאֶרֶץ מִצְרָיִם
אֲנִי ה׳ אֱלֹקיכֶם.

For the children of Israel are servants to Me;
they are My servants, whom I took out of
the land of Egypt. I am Hashem, your God.

Vayikra 25:55

Rashi explains that the reason behind this verse is that "My contract came first." Even as the nations of the world rose to power and enslaved us, they were never our true Master. Our contract with Hashem preceded them. He is and will always be our One and only boss.

Slavery can come in many different sizes and packages. There were times in history when we were physically enslaved, and there were times in history that we were emotionally or religiously enslaved. Then we have times, like today, that we have freedom of speech, freedom of religion, and lives that are safe and secure. Yet, we can still be enslaved. To whom and to what? To ourselves and to our created masters.

There are those who are always concerned with what others think about them. As a result, they feel a constant need to impress. Whether it is the house, the clothing, the weddings, or the camps, they have no rest. Others are enslaved to their boss. They think that since he signs the checks, they must bow to him and to his every whim and desire. As a result, they are constantly on edge, not able to give their own families the attention that they need and deserve. Others are enslaved to their desires. They need to fulfill all their desires at hand until the desires take them over and there is no room left in their minds and in their hearts for anything else. There is no space for their wife, their job, their children, or Hashem. We all know the destruction that follows.

My Rav, Rabbi Moshe Weinberger, encourages us by pointing out the path to freedom from this form of slavery. We must remind ourselves that we are already in contract with a Master, a contract that came before all other forms of slavery. By becoming enslaved to our bosses or our desires or our reputation, there is a breach of contract. We have prior commitments. This is not a choice; rather it is an obligation. We don't break a contract.

> *Rebbetzin Esther Jungreis was once sitting on an airplane next to a young man who was not yet observant. When the meals were being served, the Rebbetzin turned to the young man and exclaimed, "You cannot eat that, it is not kosher." The man was not convinced and was slightly annoyed with this little woman telling him what to do. But she did not let up. She then said to him, "Many years ago on Mount Sinai you signed a contract; you signed that you would keep the Torah. You can't break the contract that you signed!"*
>
> *Many years later, a man approached the Rebbetzin. This man was dressed in a clearly religious fashion. He said, "Do you recognize me?"*
>
> *"No," she responded, "I don't."*
>
> *He then proceeded to tell her that he was the young man that had once sat next to her on that plane, and the impact her words had on him brought him to where he had reached.*

May we merit to remember who we work for and who we signed a contract with. This will give us the ability to properly balance all of our lives' commitments.

Bechukosai

NOT ENOUGH TIME
IN THE DAY?!

אִם בְּחֻקֹּתַי תֵּלֵכוּ.

If you go My statutes.
Vayikra 26:3

Rashi explains that the mitzvah of אִם בְּחֻקֹּתַי תֵּלֵכוּ does not mean to listen to a *shiur* once in a while, or to occasionally flip through a book of *divrei Torah*. Rather, it means "to toil." A sincere, hardworking person may get scared off by this *Rashi*. "This seems so difficult; just look at the size of the double *parshiyos*! How can a working man, who needs to devote so much of his time to his job, fulfill *sh'nayim mikra v'echad targum*, learn *Daf Yomi*, and so much more than that? Toiling in Torah is a constant mitzvah as well; how is one to find the time and energy in the day to fulfill this *pasuk*?"

I think that the answer lies in this week's "partner *parashah*," namely, פָּרָשַׁת בְּהַר. The Torah gives us the mitzvah of *shemittah*—to stop working for an entire year, which then sets back the farmer even more. There are kids to feed, bills to pay, and the farmer just closes up shop. How can one properly fulfill this difficult mitzvah?

Yet, we know that *shemittah* brings blessing. The Torah says that "I will ordain My blessing for you in the sixth year so that it shall yield

121

a crop sufficient for three years." The year that we do not work brings *berachah*. The Torah is telling us that when we follow in His way, not only will we not lose, we will gain!

Furthermore, when we accept our true mission and see it as our real job in life, everything takes on a new perspective.

Rav Yitzchak Zilberstein relates the following story in *Aleinu Leshabei'ach*:

> *The Chafetz Chaim once spent hours of tremendous effort into understanding a difficult sugya, and afterwards he wrote one-and-a-half lines of the Mishnah Berurah. His son-in-law, who had been learning with him, asked him, "When people learn this sefer, will they know how much effort went into these few lines?"*
>
> *The Chafetz Chaim answered with another story: A father and son were sent to Siberia to pave new roads as per the Czar's command. After a hard day of work, the son asked his father, "When people will travel these roads, will they know how much sweat and hard work we put into every foot and every inch?" The father answered with two words, "Czar Papushka (Czar, our father)!"*
>
> *The father was teaching his son that it meant no difference to him what others will think. He said, "I have just one goal in mind—to fulfill the will of the Czar."*
>
> *"That," said the Chafetz Chaim, "is my intention when I write this sefer—to do the will of our Father in Heaven! Nothing else makes a difference to me."*

The same is true with all that we do. It is to please Hashem. He commanded, and we do. That is the greatest reason and explanation for every mitzvah, as the name implies—mitzvah means commandment.

So, even a difficult mitzvah like *shemittah* becomes easier. We put aside our *cheshbonos* and difficulties to do the will of Hashem. The belief that this is our calling gives a person the strength to persevere in the hardest of times. Furthermore, it allows us to feel fortunate to carry out His holy mission. We understand that we are His emissaries and are honored to live up to that. This is living a life of עֲמֵלוּת.

May we all be *zocheh* to heed to the call of our Father in Heaven and proclaim that all that we toil and do is for Hashem, our Papushka!

Sefer Bamidbar

Bamidbar

DOES THAT STAR-SPANGLED BANNER YET WAVE?

אִישׁ עַל דִּגְלוֹ בְאֹתֹת לְבֵית אֲבֹתָם
יַחֲנוּ בְּנֵי יִשְׂרָאֵל מִנֶּגֶד סָבִיב לְאֹהֶל
מוֹעֵד יַחֲנוּ.

*The children of Israel shall encamp each
man by his division with the flag staffs
of their fathers' house; some distance from
the Tent of Meeting they shall encamp.*

Bamidbar 2:2

When the Torah describes the formation of B'nei Yisrael under the flags in the desert, it gives us the details of the tribes' divisions into groups. When the *pesukim* list the three *shevatim* in each group, each *shevet* is prefaced with a *vav*, meaning "and," such as, "and camping with *shevet* Gad," or "and near him..." The only exception is in *Bamidbar* 2:7, when the *pesukim* list the group of Yehudah, Yissachar, and Zevulun. As the *pasuk* goes from Yissachar to Zevulun, it just states מַטֵּה זְבוּלֻן, the tribe of Zevulun. Why doesn't it say "**and** the tribe of Zevulun (וּמַטֵּה זְבוּלֻן)," like it does by all the others? Why is there no connecting *vav*?

127

We know that a special and unique partnership exists between *shivtei* Yissachar and Zevulun. Yissachar sat and learned Torah while Zevulun financed them. Zevulun supported Yissachar with their physical and financial needs so that they could stay immersed in their Torah study. This partnership is so authentic and so productive to the point that they become one; that is, that there is no "and" between them. Yissachar cannot learn without the support of Zevulun, and Zevulun cannot work without the Torah of Yissachar.

The world cannot exist without Torah, and at the same time, those learning Torah cannot exist without the basic needs of life. "אִם אֵין קֶמַח אֵין תּוֹרָה, אִם אֵין תּוֹרָה אֵין קֶמַח—Without flour, there is no Torah; without Torah, there is no flour."[1]

I know a man who is very connected to this concept. For example, many times when he is about to close a deal, he sets aside a certain percentage to go to a specific tzedakah organization. That organization benefits from the money, and his business benefits by being successful. They are one!

If an investor comes to you with an idea that potentially can be mutually beneficial, i.e., it's a deal that you both can gain from, you don't view him as an outsider or as a taker; you view him as an equal. You are both gaining from this partnership. If we understand tzedakah this way, we will no longer look at those who are learning or those collecting for a yeshiva as inferior. By giving tzedakah to them, we become partners in a mutually beneficial relationship. With an investor, you may lose and you may gain. That's why it's an investment. However, when supporting those who learn Torah, you will have 100 percent returns as a result of this transaction.

May we merit a true understanding of the depth of the partnership that exists between those who learn Torah and those who support Torah learning. We will then proudly wave our flags, regardless of which camp we find ourselves in.

---

1   *Avos* 3:17.

Naso

NANANAKISHKISH

וַיֹּאמֶר ה׳ אֶל מֹשֶׁה נָשִׂיא אֶחָד לַיּוֹם
נָשִׂיא אֶחָד לַיּוֹם יַקְרִיבוּ אֶת קָרְבָּנָם
לַחֲנֻכַּת הַמִּזְבֵּחַ.

And Hashem said to Moshe: One chieftain
each day, one chieftain each day, shall
present his offering for the dedication
of the altar.

Bamidbar 7:11

We all know the obvious and apparent question: Why does the Torah write seventy-nine *pesukim* repeating the *korban* that each *nasi* brought? Why not write the *korban* once and let us know that they all brought that *korban*?

Rabbi Yissachar Frand points out a simple but beautiful lesson. While it is true that all the *korbanos* were the same, the repetition of each *shevet* and its *korban* highlights something unique and specific. Each one was beautiful; each one was meaningful. Why? Because none of them were trying to outdo the other. Their intentions were pure and holy. They wanted to bring a donation for the *Mishkan*, and they wanted their donation to look like everybody else's. Nobody was trying to look better or outdo the other.

This theme can connect to an earlier event. When everybody was donating material to build the *Mishkan*, the Nesi'im said, "Whatever is missing, we will bring." It turns out that nothing was missing, so Hashem did them a favor and brought the *avnei miluim* and the *avnei shoham* to them so that they could have what to donate.

We know that their attitude was not the best way they could have behaved. That is why a letter was taken out of their name. Why was it considered wrong?

First, when someone is excited to do a mitzvah, they immediately jump at the opportunity to do it and do not become so calculated.

Second, if *chas v'shalom* there would have been a lot of building materials still needed after B'nei Yisrael brought their donation, that would have fallen onto the Nesi'im as they accepted. Were they so sure that they could fill that gap? Accepting such a responsibility potentially implied that they were higher than the rest of Klal Yisrael. "We can fill your lack; we've got you covered," so to speak. It sounds haughty.

So, they didn't repeat their mistake. They quickly jumped at this new opportunity to give, and they all gave the same—as equals.

How much energy are we investing into outdoing others? Whether it's trying to make more money, build a nicer home, throw a fancier *simchah*, or go on a more exotic vacation? Do we direct others to help them to be the best that they can be, or are we too preoccupied with making sure that our car looks just a little bit better than the car of our next-door neighbor?

There was a holy Jew, Reb Shloimy Gross. Whenever a *chessed* opportunity came his way, or rather whenever he searched for ways to do *chessed*, that became to him the deal of the century. He would make phone calls for people, set up meetings, and lend his car—whatever it would take to make sure that another person could become successful. It almost seemed as though he did not work for himself as he applied so much of his time and effort to make others shine.

May we merit to always look at our brothers with a kind eye and never feel a need to outdo or outshine anybody else.

Behaalosecha

ALL FOR ONE
AND ONE FOR ALL

דַּבֵּר אֶל אַהֲרֹן וְאָמַרְתָּ אֵלָיו
בְּהַעֲלֹתְךָ אֶת הַנֵּרֹת אֶל מוּל פְּנֵי
הַמְּנוֹרָה יָאִירוּ שִׁבְעַת הַנֵּרוֹת.

*Speak to Aharon and say to him: "When you
light the lamps, the seven lamps shall cast
their light toward the face of the Menorah."*
Bamidbar 8:2

he Menorah that the *pasuk* is speaking of refers to the middle light. It is the long central part of the Menorah that does not branch out—the beam that supports the rest of the Menorah. Thus, the *Seforno* explains as follows: The three lights that branch out to the right represent those who learn Torah and devote their time and energy to prayer and other spiritual pursuits. The three that branch out to the left represent those who are involved in business and supporting their fellow brothers who are immersed in Torah. The *pasuk* is teaching us that when the two sides are facing the middle—meaning when they have the same intention to do the will of Hashem—then יָאִירוּ שִׁבְעַת הַנֵּרֹת, they will all shine and the name of Hashem will be glorified.

131

This is why the Menorah is hammered specifically out of one piece of gold. No matter which side of the Menorah you are on, as long as your purpose is one and the same, then you are part of this glorious Menorah.

If we internalize the message of the Menorah, it will allow us to see the intrinsic importance of every single Jew. Everyone in their unique way is fulfilling their purpose. I don't see myself as greater than others; I see myself as a teammate, as a partner with the candle to my right and the candle to my left. We are all carved out from the same source; all of our souls are a portion of Hashem above. Just as the Menorah was hammered into different shapes and sides, so too, the Jewish nation has within it many people with many roles. Just like the Menorah radiated light, so too, all the Jewish People have a shared common goal to let the light of our soul glow and come together with the souls of others to radiate the light of the *Shechinah* and Hashem Himself.

> *One Shabbos, toward the end of davening, a Yerushalmi Yid let his friends know that he was giving a Kiddush in their shtiebel for a reason unknown to them. In middle of the Kiddush, he showed up dressed in full IDF uniform along with his four-year-old son. He then proceeded to let them know why he was making this Kiddush.*
>
> *"I grew up in a house void of Torah and mitzvos. Religion was unwanted in the home. I joined the army and grew in the ranks until I was leading an elite unit of seven hundred soldiers. In the beginning of the Yom Kippur War, the country needed time to call up the reserves, as they were not prepared. They called me in to see if we could go up north to hold off the enemy (although we were terribly outnumbered) until reinforcements would arrive. They said we should expect a very high number of casualties. We accepted the mission. Miraculously, we only lost thirty men—much fewer than anticipated, but still, thirty too many.*
>
> *"After Sukkos, we had a commemoration ceremony at our base. Seven hundred chairs were set up; thirty of them had pictures*

on them of the fallen chayalim. I asked a rabbi to come speak, and I told him that I need him to give chizuk to the unit. That was what I told him.

"*I spoke first and lauded the unit for their intense training and capabilities, which showed itself on the battlefield. No mention of Hashem. Then, as I prepared to call up the rabbi, I posed a question to him. 'How could it be,' I asked, 'that all of us risked our lives to go fight, and many lost their lives, while all of you charedim stayed back in the safety of your home! Where were you when we were being shot at?'*

"*With that said, I called up the rabbi. Really, I had not called him for chizuk, rather I called him to let out my anger on him and all his type.*

"*He thought for a moment, and then began to speak: 'You all acknowledge that what happened was not natural,' he said. 'Enemy bombs that never exploded and single tanks defeating hundreds was not because you trained. It was obviously a power from Above. Well, every Sukkos, the yeshivos take a break. At the onset of the war, all the Roshei Hayeshiva decided that there would be no break. All the yeshivos would stay open so they could learn and pray that we win the war. Where were we? We were partnering with you! We both did our part, and Hashem brought us a miraculous salvation!'*

"*He finished speaking to a very loud applause from the crowd. I was very unsettled, so I decided to go for a jog. I left the base, and I ran. I stopped at the first yeshiva I saw. I went in and found a young man learning.*

"'*Where were you during the Sukkos break?' I asked him.*

"'*Sukkos break?' he said. 'Not this year! We were all in yeshiva to help our brothers on the battlefield!'*

"*I left and ran to another yeshiva. Again, I asked a young man about his break and got a similar response. 'Break?! We were in yeshiva fighting!'*

"Rabbosai, that was many years ago," said the Yerushalmi Yid. "Now, I am sending my son to start cheder this week. I want him to know where true power comes from. I want him to know who is always in control—Hashem and the Torah. That is the reason for the Kiddush."

May we all be *zocheh* to realize the value and need of all Yidden and what they do. In that merit, we will all join together and **shine** toward the center and purpose of all, i.e., Hashem.

FOMO

וַיֹּאמְרוּ הָאֲנָשִׁים הָהֵמָּה אֵלָיו אֲנַחְנוּ
טְמֵאִים לְנֶפֶשׁ אָדָם לָמָּה נִגָּרַע
לְבִלְתִּי הַקְרִיב אֶת קָרְבַּן ה׳ בְּמֹעֲדוֹ
בְּתוֹךְ בְּנֵי יִשְׂרָאֵל.

Those men said to him, "We are ritually
unclean [because of contact] with a dead
person; [but] why should we be excluded
so as not to bring the offering of Hashem
in its appointed time, with all the children
of Yisrael?"

Bamidbar 9:7

When Moshe Rabbeinu spoke with Hashem regarding the request of those Jews who had been *tamei* at the time the B'nei Yisrael brought the *Korban Pesach* in the *midbar*, Hashem decided that they can have a second chance—the *Korban Pesach Sheini*. This wasn't only offered to those who were *tamei*, but also to those people who may have been too far away at the time of Pesach. This second dispensation is more than what Klal Yisrael asked for; this second group hadn't been brought up in the original request.

We see an illuminating concept from what took place. If, for whatever reason, a Jew can't do a mitzvah, and it seems that there is nothing he can do about it, he may think that he's missed his chance and it's all over. From what took place here, we see how this Jew can have hope that there is always something that can be done about it. He can feel bad about it, and he can wish that he had an opportunity for that mitzvah. If he truly feels pain over his loss, the feeling itself will benefit him greatly.

The Jews that were impure were not required to bring the *Korban Pesach*. Halachically speaking, they were off the hook. Yet, they yearned to serve their Creator; they had a deep desire to bring up the *korban* to Hashem. And what happened? Not only did they get a second chance for their specific situation, Hashem actually added on even more that others who found themselves on a long trip or under circumstances that made it impossible to perform the *korban* would also be given another chance. Hashem was showing them and us that our desire to want to do good benefits not only us but also the entire Jewish nation as well, as we see that in the end they got more than they asked for.

> *A friend of mine was in yeshiva when he passed the office of his rebbi, who seemed to be searching for something. He asked his rebbi what he was looking for so that he could be of assistance in the search. Before my friend even helped, his rebbi found the sefer he had been looking for and immediately thanked my friend.*
>
> *"But I didn't do anything," the talmid responded.*
>
> *The rebbi answered, "The fact that you cared and wanted to help helped me find the sefer I was looking for."*

When a Jew wants to do something and he desires something, it brings great *yeshuos*. We have a special charge as Jews to constantly be מְצַפִּים לִישׁוּעָה—hoping for the Salvation. Aside from the Torah and the good deeds that we are supposed to do to help hasten the redemption, we are also supposed to want and hope for it. This is yet another example of how the feelings and the desires of a Jew are crucial, beneficial, holy, and powerful.

I once heard a Rav say that if somebody is very busy at work but he truly wishes he had more time for his learning, through his sincere feelings he can change his situation. And even if he doesn't see actual change, the yearning itself is a holy level.

May we all merit to realize the greatness of every mitzvah to the point that it becomes our truest, most sincere inner desire. The term that kids use these days is called FOMO—Fear of Missing Out. May we always experience *the fear of missing out* with regard to the mitzvos, and in that merit may Hashem have constant patience with us and give us all a second chance, even if sometimes we are far away.

Shelach

POSITIVITY BIAS

וַיַּרְאוּם אֶת פְּרִי הָאָרֶץ.

And they showed them the fruit of the land.
Bamidbar 13:26

The intention of the spies was to show everybody, as *Rashi* says, that "just as the fruits are uniquely different, so too the people are, and therefore there is no way that we will be able to overcome them."

Now, we know in truth that the fact that the fruits of the lands were so large was the result of the great blessing of Eretz Yisrael. It took eight people to carry one cluster of grapes; one person could only carry one fig! That seems unbelievable. Why would anybody think that seeing something like this could be anything but fabulous? Yet, the spies chose to see it in a different way. They viewed the large fruits as negative, bad, and dangerous.

This is indeed a big eye-opener for us. Many times in life, there are two people who can see the exact same thing. They can experience the same event, yet they will have inverse reactions. One will view the item or experience as good or even great, while the other will view it in a bad and negative light. It may be that both are true. One decides to focus on the positive, while the other on the negative.

The Midrash compares a person who speaks gossip to a fly. Just as a fly will land on a person exactly where they have a scab or dried blood and not on any clean surface, so too are the ones who speak bad. They choose to find the bad that is within a person and a situation, and they "zoom in" and land on that.

There can be two people at the same family *simchah*. One can be enjoying the family, the music and having a very nice time, while right next to him the other can be anything but happy. His seat was not in the perfect location, the speaker was not to his liking, and the meat tasted too dry. It is the same event, and yet two people are experiencing it in completely different ways.

We can take it a step further. As we've mentioned earlier, everything in our world has a true and meaningful purpose, and it is our duty to use our experiences in the right way. For instance, in our occupation, two people can be sitting in cubicles right next to each other in the same office, working on the same project, and they can have completely different experiences. While one man is viewing his work as tedious and unpleasant—a waste of what he can truly be doing with his time—the other man is choosing to find the positive in what is being done. He repeats to himself, "I am helping my family; I am doing good in my specific field of work; I am serving Hashem with the tools that He has given me today." Two people, same line of work. One is constantly serving Hashem, while the other creates a self-made barrier; his cubicle is keeping Godliness out of the picture.

I was once part of a group trying to put together a very large deal. It would have brought in a very nice profit. A lot of time and energy was invested. We were sure that we had the deal. At the last minute we lost the deal to a competitor. There were a lot of intense reactions—the type that they probably regretted after they calmed down. There were a few people, though, who remained calm and collected and showed their true *bitachon*. They did not lose. A few years later, when the transaction came due again, they got the deal plus more deals going forward from that client. One transaction, many reactions!

May we all merit to see only the good in our God-given world. May we have the insight to realize how we can utilize it all to serve Hashem, and may we all very soon be shown the most beautiful land ever, the city of gold, Yerushalayim Ir Hakodesh!

Korach

MAY WE BLOSSOM

וַיַּנַּח מֹשֶׁה אֶת הַמַּטֹּת לִפְנֵי ה׳
בְּאֹהֶל הָעֵדֻת.

*And Moshe placed the staffs before Hashem
in the Tent of the Testimony.*

Bamidbar 17:22

After the episode with Korach and his followers and their subsequent punishment, Hashem did something to eliminate further complaints. Each *shevet* was to give a staff to Moshe with their tribal name engraved on it. The staff that would begin to sprout would prove to all that they were chosen for Hashem's special service. The *pasuk* says, "and Moshe placed the staffs before Hashem, in the *Mishkan*." According to how the *Rashbam* learns the next *pasuk*, when Moshe took the staffs out, everyone saw that the staff of Levi had blossomed while the others remained the same. Then, after everybody saw the blossoms, it began to sprout a bud, and the almonds ripened.

The Gateshead Rosh Yeshiva asks why the entire process couldn't have take place in front of B'nei Yisrael? Why did the blossoming have to initially begin in the *Mishkan*?

He answers that the Torah is teaching us an important lesson about how crucial beginnings are. How we start a process has an impact on all subsequent growth. It was necessary for the staff to begin its growth לִפְנֵי ה׳—in *kedushah* and *taharah*. It is only because of this initial stage that it was able to prosper in a different environment.

Our source, our *shoresh*, our roots, are what we build everything else upon. Similarly, if a tree has taken root in Eretz Yisrael, yet the branches are leaning out to *chutz la'aretz*, the owner is still required to separate *terumos* and *maaseros*. Why? Because of its source, Eretz Yisrael. This is where everything comes from.

The same is true for us. "Man is like the tree of the field." Where are we rooted, and what is our life-sustaining force? Once we choose to be rooted in the *Mishkan*, i.e., in holiness, then we build our entire lives—our sprouts, our blossoms, and our fruit—from this holy source.

As we branch out into our day to the office, the train, the city, we must stay connected to our source and lifeline. The home that we have built for ourselves and the davening and learning that we started our day with should keep us rooted all day! And more! The realization that there is purpose and holiness in every moment and person should give us constant direction.

May we merit to attain the clarity of where we come from and who we truly are—*banim la'Makom*. May our lives be filled with beautiful flowers and fruits that can proudly fill the garden of Hashem.

Chukas

TOTAL IMMERSION

זֹאת הַתּוֹרָה אָדָם כִּי יָמוּת בְּאֹהֶל
כָּל הַבָּא אֶל הָאֹהֶל וְכָל אֲשֶׁר בָּאֹהֶל
יִטְמָא שִׁבְעַת יָמִים.

This is the law: if a man dies in a tent,
anyone entering the tent and anything in
the tent shall be unclean for seven days.

Bamidbar 19:14

The above verse was said regarding the laws of *tumah* emanating from a dead body. The Gemara says the following: "אָמַר רַבִּי שִׁמְעוֹן בֶּן לָקִישׁ אֵין דִּבְרֵי תוֹרָה מִתְקַיְּמִין אֶלָּא בְּמִי שֶׁמֵּמִית עַצְמוֹ עָלֶיהָ—The Torah can only have an existence by one who dies over it."[1] What does this mean?

If somebody is involved in a very big business deal that can earn him a nice profit, and there is a lot of work that needs to be done to make sure that the deal happens, time is of the essence. He does not want to lose this deal. What happens at lunchtime? He does not even realize he is hungry! What about the coffee on his desk? It is cold! What about when his wife or kids are calling? He has no time for them! After this deal is closed, he plans on having plenty of time. Now, however, it is as

---

1   *Gittin* 57b.

though the world is sleeping or dead. All else stands still as he is focused on only one thing—the deal.

When we care about something so much, we find ourselves hyper-focused while everything else takes a backseat. Even the parts of life that we typically enjoy, such as a well-prepared lunch or a beautiful spring day, are temporarily put on hold until we finish that which we are so caught up in.

There is no greater deal in life than the world of Torah. It reaps us benefits worth much more than the millions of this world. Its rewards last for eternity. Just as anything truly important takes precedence over everything else, all the more so in the world of Torah. It cannot have continuous existence unless we consider everything else dead, so to speak, or on hold while we are preoccupied with the greatest deal of our lifetime.

The *parashah* tells us about the *parah adumah*, the purification process from impurity. One of its laws is that it can never have had any burden on it, i.e., it never carried a yoke. The greatest purity is the *mikvah* of Torah. If we can cast off all other burdens—the constant email, our ringing phone, our excessive need to fulfill pleasure—all of which weigh us down, then we can properly live a life of Torah. But as long as the yoke is ever-present, it will be very hard for us to enjoy the gift of Torah. The *parah adumah* is the *chukas haTorah*—the law of the Torah. Simply put, when our ultimate burden and responsibility is Torah and *avodas Hashem*, it does not just help us learn. It gives us perspective and direction in everything else that we are involved in. Renewed strength and new meaning are found in what we do day-to-day. The world on its own is "dead," so to speak, and we infuse it with value when Torah takes priority.

Rabbi Zev Leff of Modi'in never set out to be a star—he just wanted to learn Torah. The Rosh Yeshiva became a sensation when a stadium camera caught him learning at the Israel-Scotland game in Glasgow.

Rav Leff was apparently visiting his daughter, Rebbetzin Sarah Bodenheim, and accompanied members of her family to the game. In a clip that tore through the Orthodox world, the Sky News camera panned to Rav Leff's family just after Israel scored its first goal. Rav Leff was snug in a coat, scarf, holding a sefer with a weathered-looking cover. The title was not legible.

"I think he missed the goal," one of the commentators lamented, as Rav Leff was seen buried in his sefer. The camera stayed squarely on Rav Leff, who was immobile except for his eyeballs, seemingly unaware of the commotion around him. Next to him, people who appear to be his wife, daughter, and grandchildren watched the game.

"Must be a good read," another commentator chuckles. Must be.

Rav Leff eventually looked up and penetrated the camera with a glance that said, "I will never, ever be shamed over my holy study. No! Not even by the charming Scottish sports commentators."

This is a true example that the world on its own is "dead," so to speak, and we infuse it with value when Torah takes priority.

May we merit a level of concentration and intensity in our *avodas ha'kodesh* that will seep into everything else that we do and ultimately give life, not death, to whatever we are involved with.

Balak

IN IT FOR THE MONEY

וַיֹּאמֶר אֱלֹקִים אֶל בִּלְעָם לֹא תֵלֵךְ
עִמָּהֶם לֹא תָאֹר אֶת הָעָם
כִּי בָרוּךְ הוּא.

*Hashem said to Bilaam, "You shall not go
with them! You shall not curse the people
because they are blessed."*

Bamidbar 22:12

When Bilaam was initially offered a hefty sum to curse the B'nei Yisrael, although he wanted to, Hashem told him "No." Again, messengers came and offered him a heftier sum, and although Hashem then gave him permission to go, Hashem sent an angel to stop him. Then, Hashem turned each potential curse that was given into a *berachah*. After all this, Bilaam gets killed by the sword.

We say in *Ashrei*, "רְצוֹן יְרֵאָיו יַעֲשֶׂה וְאֶת שַׁוְעָתָם יִשְׁמַע וְיוֹשִׁיעֵם—Do the will of those who fear You and listen to their cry and save them."[1] But if Hashem has already fulfilled our *ratzon*—will, why does He also have to hear our cry?

---

1   *Tehillim* 145:19.

Sometimes we have a particular request in mind, something that we think will be good for us, but it may not be the case. It could be that we would be better off without it. There are times that it will be much better if Hashem just hears our cry, and then He can decide what we need. Our *ratzon* may not always be the proper solution. Many times in life, if something that we pursue doesn't go through, we think that we've failed. We didn't get the deal, we didn't get into the seminary of our choice, we didn't get put on the team, etc. However, the truth is that the love of Hashem guides us; He knows what is truly good for us.

A parent will take a cookie away from their two-year-old child right before supper so that the child will eat some healthy food. In the child's immature mind, the parent is mean—they took my delicious cookie away, it was what I wanted, it was my desire. We are also immature children, so to speak. There are many cookies in life that we truly want. Sometimes He takes them away for our good. To us, it looked like we failed, but He knows better; it is for our health.

David HaMelech says that "אַךְ טוֹב וָחֶסֶד יִרְדְּפוּנִי כָּל יְמֵי חַיָּי וְשַׁבְתִּי בְּבֵית ה'—לְאֹרֶךְ יָמִים—May good and kindness chase me..."[2] There are times in life that we are actually running away from that which is good for us. We think that we've figured it out. Yet, we can be heading toward failure. We ask Hashem that His goodness chase us down, even though we might be running the wrong way.

Hashem gave Bilaam so many chances. He was a wicked man trying to curse B'nei Yisrael, and he was still given opportunities by Hashem to chase that which would be better for him. The next time in business something does not go the way we anticipated, as long as we did our *chelek*, what was expected of us, we can be comforted. If this is what ended up happening, this must be the plan of God. This must be the best outcome. Nobody complains when money comes in an unexpected way, even when no effort was put in. Why not? Because if it came my way, it must be for me! The same is true the other way around.

---

2   Ibid. 23:6.

May we all merit to live a life filled with obvious blessing, and may we chase after good and be chased by it as well. May be merit to see the day when the cry of all generations will be ultimately heard.

OUR DOWN-TO-EARTH
GOODNESS

וַיֹּאמֶר אֱלֹקִים אֶל בִּלְעָם לֹא תֵלֵךְ
עִמָּהֶם לֹא תָאֹר אֶת הָעָם
כִּי בָרוּךְ הוּא.

Hashem said to Bilaam, "You shall not go
with them! You shall not curse the people
because they are blessed."

Bamidbar 22:12

O riginally, when Bilaam was offered to curse B'nei Yisrael, Hashem told him not to go. The second time, however, when Bilaam said, "If you pay me a house filled with silver and gold, I cannot go against Hashem," then Hashem told him he should go. As *Rashi* explains, "If you think you will get money, then you can go with them to curse B'nei Yisrael." What changed? Why now did Hashem tell Bilaam that he can go?

Rabbi Yissachar Frand answers that doing something *lishmah*—with pure intentions, is a very dangerous endeavor. Doing something "*lo lishmah*" for money is OK, and it is not so bad. What does this mean? Shouldn't it be the opposite? In a perfect world, yes, it should be the opposite. However, reality teaches us that when one claims he is doing something with pure intention, we have reason to be concerned. There must be some ulterior motive, bad intention, or evil plan. However, when money is involved, although it is not a pure intention, it is still only as bad as it sounds; it is for money. You know exactly what you are getting with no hidden dangers lurking. If a stranger were to do a very big favor for you, it would make you nervous. What is coming next? What expectation does he have? However, if he charges you, then all is good. Simple and clear—it was for money and for nothing else. Although we strive for sincerity, for pureness of heart, for real service of Hashem, we cannot fool ourselves. We must know who we truly are and not get carried away. That could, God forbid, lead us to act in a way that is not in the best interest of ourselves, others, and especially Hashem.

One need not feel bad when involved in the mundane parts of life. On the contrary; acknowledge that this is what Hashem wants of us. It may not be so mundane after all.

The Mishnah says that יָפֶה תַלְמוּד תּוֹרָה עִם דֶּרֶךְ אֶרֶץ.[1] This doesn't mean that Torah is less important and that we are able to relax when it comes to our Torah learning. Rather, it means that we should know who it is that has an obligation to learn—a person of this earth! Not a *malach*, a celestial being, but rather, a man with all his manly desires. We were created "*b'derech eretz*"; we were created from the very earth upon which we stand. And it is specifically this living, breathing, earthly, and materialistic man that Hashem desires Torah from. יָפֶה—how beautiful is Torah, עִם דֶּרֶךְ אֶרֶץ—from an earthly being.

May we merit to take all the "*she'lo lishmah*" of this world and direct it to "*lishmah*"—the name of Hashem.

---

1   *Avos* 2:2.

Pinchas

WHAT IS MY CALLING?

עַל פִּי הַגּוֹרָל תֵּחָלֵק נַחֲלָתוֹ.

The inheritance shall be apportioned
according to the lot.
Bamidbar 26:56

Eretz Yisrael was divided in a miraculous way. Aside from the *nissim* involved in conquering it, the actual division was quite amazing.

Rashi explains from a Gemara that Eliezer, who wore the *Urim V'Tumim*, announced with *ruach ha'kodesh* which *shevet* would receive which land portion in the upcoming *goral*. Then, the twelve *shevatim* were written down and placed in a box along with the twelve land portions. Then, the *goral* would call out the results and say, "I, the lottery, declare this portion for this *shevet*."[1] Miracle upon miracle!

On a similar note, we know that before a person is born, a *bas kol* calls out who we will marry and what field will be ours as well. Not only were the tribal portions decided by Hashem, but one's individual *chelek* is decided as well. Many parts of our life get an announcement; it is officially proclaimed.

---

1   *Rashi* loc cit., citing *Bava Basra* 123a–b.

When we realize this, it helps us stay focused on acquiring and maintaining our portion. The grass is only greener on the other side when we have even a slight thought that perhaps it can and should be our lot. By listening to the *bas kol*, we have the peace of mind to pursue and enhance the *chelek* that is ours.

This will not only help us in our physical life. If we understand that we have a *chelek*, a charge in terms of spiritual *middos*, we will have much clarity there as well. Let us explain:

Pinchas was the only one who took matters into his own hands by killing Zimri and Kozbi, and by doing so he stopped the plague. Even Moshe Rabbeinu forgot (so to speak) the halachah, as Rashi there states.

What gives a person the strength to act alone with no other backing?

Pinchas heard the cry of מִי לַה' אֵלָי. He was from the family of Leviim. He knew exactly what his *chelek* was—his job in this world. When someone hears their calling, it gives them the ability to go against the tide. Nobody else would have dared kill a *Nasi b'Yisrael*. There was opposition after Pinchas did this because many couldn't understand how he had the audacity to kill a *nasi*! Hashem cleared all doubts and granted Pinchas "The Treaty of Peace." For killing he gets peace? What is the *middah k'neged middah*?

Peace is clarity and *shalom*; peace is the same *lashon* as *shaleim*—complete. There is no greater peace of mind than knowing that you are following the call of Hashem, the call that He proclaimed specifically for you. This leads us to live a life of *sheleimus*—completion.

My daughter once came home late and went out to pick up some dinner. It was late, and the eateries were closed. She came to Holy Shnitzel and, to her dismay, they were closing up as well. "Do you have anything?" she asked. The manager said that he was sorry but the kitchen was already closed. "How about a pickle? Anything?" The manager then realized that there was an order that had not been picked up. "Here," he said, "take this." He handed her a bag. In it contained none other than her favorite sandwich from Holy Shnitzel. Not only that, he gave it to her for free!

Hashem takes care of us and sends us all our *chelek*, down to the smallest detail. If it is meant for us, we will get it! That sandwich was truly a Holy Toasty (the actual name of that sandwich)!

May we merit to hear the *bas kol* of what Hashem wants our *chelek* to be, and may we truly be able to say "אַשְׁרֵינוּ מַה טוֹב חֶלְקֵנוּ—How fortunate are we, how good is our lot!"

Matos

WORD POWER

לֹא יַחֵל דְּבָרוֹ.

He shall not violate his word.
Bamidbar 30:3

This verse is referring to a person who makes a vow. *Rashi* adds, "don't make your words non-sacred." We see from this *Rashi* the strength of words; words are holy! If I keep my word, then my word remains *kadosh*. Only if I break my word does it become *chullin*, non-holy.

The Gemara asks that there seems to be a contradiction between two well-known *pesukim*. In one *pasuk*, it states that "Hashem owns the land and all that is in it,"[1] and in another *pasuk* it says, "Land was given to man."[2] Who owns the land? Man or God?

It depends, answers the Gemara. Before we make a *berachah*, it belongs to Hashem, and after we make a *berachah*, it becomes ours.[3] When we declare that it is all from Hashem and that He gave it to us for our enjoyment, we are allowed to benefit from it. We are using it for its intended purpose. That Gemara goes so far as to say that one who

---

1   *Tehillim* 24:1.
2   Ibid. 115:16.
3   *Berachos* 35a.

153

doesn't make a *berachah* is stealing! The Owner doesn't allow him to use it for any other purpose than a Godly intention!

If you were to lend someone a car with the condition that he not drive it on dirt roads, then if he chooses to drive on dirt roads, he has stolen from you. You had a condition, and permission was not granted in that situation.

The Gemara then says that one who benefits from this world without a *berachah*, it is as if they were מָעַל. Now, this prohibition exists when something is owned by the Beis Hamikdash, for it is holy—it is *hekdesh*. If one takes personal benefit from it, they have committed the sin of *me'ilah*.

If we apply this sin to one who does not make a *berachah*, we are acknowledging that everything in this world is holy, and anything that is *hekdesh* and is not treated properly can turn into *me'ilah*.

My friend was once with a group of teenagers on a school trip. At one point, he took the microphone and shared a *d'var Torah* with the group—nothing prepared, just a thought that he had. After placing the mic back down, the non-Jewish driver commented, "That was great! Who wrote that speech?"

"It was just something that I was thinking of," my friend responded. The driver could not understand.

That driver made it so clear to us. Our words are holy. They are a gift that we as children of Hashem are gifted with.

Let us realize the strength of our words; they have the power to create holiness. What we say throughout the day, to our colleagues, at meetings, on the phone, or at lunch—the words and tone that we use can bring others and ourselves to an awareness of the goal of all the blessings that we have. All of our interactions and words can be holy.

May we merit sanctifying our words, our thoughts, and our actions so that, ultimately, what belongs to Hashem will be gifted to us.

NOT BECOMING SPOILED
WITH SPOILS

וַיֵּצְאוּ מֹשֶׁה וְאֶלְעָזָר הַכֹּהֵן וְכָל נְשִׂיאֵי
הָעֵדָה לִקְרָאתָם אֶל מִחוּץ לַמַּחֲנֶה.

*Moshe, Elazar the Kohen, and all the
chieftains of the community went out to
meet them outside the camp.*

Bamidbar 31:13

After B'nei Yisrael battled and beat Midyan, they returned with all their loot. *Rashi* points out that Moshe and Elazar went out to greet them because "the lads of Yisrael were going out to grab from their booty."

Why were they grabbing? The next group of *pesukim* explain how the booty was divided amongst the nation of Yisrael. Why then would they feel a need to grab what was already coming to them?

Rashi uses the term "lads," which implies immaturity. They displayed childish behavior by grabbing. Children worry that there will not be enough pieces of pie, even when there is more than enough for all. Second, something that is precious and dear to a person has the ability to take the person over.

We sometimes fall into this childish way of acting as well. We feel a need to chase *parnassah*, run after a client, or monopolize our business because we are worried that there are too many hands in the pie. Will Hashem have enough left for me?

Just as Hashem divided the spoils amongst the nation, He divides *parnassah* amongst us as well. We go out and fight the battles, and then let Hashem decide what is ours for the taking.

This thought can give us much peace of mind. We do not have to feel that we should be over-exerting our self to do more so that we don't lose a potential deal. Hashem has plenty for all of us. No need to *chap*!

> *Someone once came to Rav Chaim Kanievsky with a real concern. He had just won the lottery and was nervous that his friends and neighbors would be jealous of him. "What should I do?" he asked. Rav Chaim asked him if he had a chavrusa in the morning. "I leave to work too early," he answered.*
>
> *"How about in the evening?" Rav Chaim then asked him.*
>
> *"I work too late, and by the time I get home, I must get to bed."*
>
> *"So, I do not understand," said Rav Chaim. "What would anyone be jealous of?"*

May we merit developing a mature attitude in regard to our *parnassah*. As much as immaturity and childish behaviors are part of the process, we hope to grow out of that mindset and develop an outlook of *emunah* and *bitachon*.

THE SPICE OF LIFE

כָּל דָּבָר אֲשֶׁר יָבֹא בָאֵשׁ תַּעֲבִירוּ
בָאֵשׁ וְטָהֵר.

*Whatever is used in fire you shall pass
through fire, and then it will be pure.*

Bamidbar 31:23

This *pasuk* is teaching us how to kasher our utensils. The *sefer Shabbos Vort* shares a beautiful lesson from the Chida with us. Every person has within them a fire of the *yetzer hara* that burns and tempts them to sin. But there is also the fire of the Torah—a fire of holiness and purity. The Gemara says, "I have created the *yetzer hara*, and I have created a Torah as its *tavlin*—antidote."[1] Through Torah study, a person can save themselves and overpower the *yetzer hara*. That is what the *pasuk* means when it says that everything that comes into the fire (of the *yetzer hara*) you shall pass through the fire (of the Torah) and it will be purified. Simply put, we must involve ourselves in the Torah to overcome the *yetzer hara*.

Let's take this a step further. If a person has tremendous passion toward a specific profession, they feel alive when they are involved in

---

1   *Kiddushin* 30b.

157

that. They have all the energy and smiles and the ability to keep going. This is their domain; they are the salesman, the doctor, the lawyer, etc. Yet, as soon as they step out of that area and go home to their family or to shul, they become a different person. Gone is the passion and energy that they had earlier. Trying to break the passion that they exhibit for their profession would be counterproductive, as it would probably break the person completely. However, utilizing and redirecting that amazing fire and energy can bring beautiful results.

For example, if a person loves being involved in sales, he can view the entire world as a potential deal. How? By realizing the great reward for doing a good deed or for davening. He can calculate the amount of time he invests into his learning portfolio. A surgeon is unbelievably meticulous and detail-oriented. That level of detail orientation can be applied to his ability to learn and know halachah and to dissect and understand parts of Torah in a very detail-oriented way. Rather than suffocating and extinguishing the fire, our goal is to use it for good.

The Gemara says that Torah is the *tavlin*. *Tavlin* also means a spice. The purpose of spices is not to change or overtake the dish; that would actually ruin the food. Rather, it is meant to bring out the potential flavor of the food. The tastes that already lie within the food can be enjoyed when it is accompanied by a specific spice. The Torah can help us not to diminish our fire but rather to use it to spice up all areas of our life and to make all areas tasteful in a holy way.

Rav Levi Yitzchak would say that the best mitzvos are the *aveiros* that we did *teshuvah* on. Why? Because we know that *teshuvah* out of love has the power to turn a sin into a good deed. When a person does a sin, there's a fire and the passion of the *yetzer hara* involved. The urge and the desires that man had can be used and channeled for the purpose of a mitzvah. Mitzvos done with that level of passion are the best mitzvos.

May we all merit to direct the fire within the *yetzer hara* to pass through the fire of the Torah, which ultimately will allow us to create and build a holy fire—a holy offering.

Masei

I'M JUST PASSING THROUGH

וַיִּסְעוּ מִקִּבְרֹת הַתַּאֲוָה וַיַּחֲנוּ בַּחֲצֵרֹת.

They journeyed from Kivros Hata'avah and
camped in Chatzeros.

Bamidbar 33:17

av Yitzchak of Vorka tells us that a powerful lesson is being hinted at in this verse. If a person wants to know the secret to overcoming the *yetzer hara* within, he must remember that this world is temporary and that its entire purpose is to prepare us for the World to Come. The *pasuk* says we can bury (*Kivros*) our desires (*Ta'avah*) by remembering that this world is merely a yard (*Chatzeros*). The purpose of the yard is just to lead you to your destination, i.e., the house, as the well-known Mishnah says, "This world is like a hallway before a palace. One who is going into the palace (Next World) prepares himself in the hallway (this world)."[1] If we take this lesson to heart, we can find success in overcoming and quieting the *yetzer hara*.

The *yetzer hara* comes to a person from many different angles. Sometimes he simply gets us involved in foolish endeavors, such as simply filling our desires. However, he sometimes takes a different

---

1   *Avos* 4:21.

approach entirely, making it seem as though there is something very important that we must invest our time and energy into. He convinces us so well that we can sometimes even claim that what we are doing is a mitzvah. We might put down others who are not taking our task as seriously as we are. To respond to both tactics, the Torah is telling us not to get too caught up. This world is only temporary. In response to the one that is running to fulfill his desires, we can tell him that they will be short-lived. In response to the person who is taking parts of this world so seriously, again, we can tell him to calm down and relax as this world is only a means to something much greater.

Although earning a *parnassah* is important, as we have a responsibility to our families, we need to take a step back. Firstly, inasmuch as that responsibility is paramount, so too is the rest of the Torah. One mitzvah should never put aside many other mitzvos. Second, we need to remember what the point of our working is and what the point of living is. Of course, it is for a greater cause—to fulfill our spiritual mission in this world. If so, no part of our work should contradict the truest mission and point of living. Third, we should not take our work too seriously, as we know that it is only a gift, and it really isn't truly our investment that is determining the outcome.

Why is it acceptable for the family member learning in Kollel to be expected to be available to come to every family *simchah* and event, while the family member in college or working is lauded for taking work so seriously by not joining the family event? He can't just take off—he is doing something important. What about the husband who gets an earful for staying out an extra few minutes in shul to learn but is encouraged to stay in the office late if it will bring in more *parnassah*? Sometimes we take parts of this temporary life a little bit too seriously.

We all know the famous *pasuk* from Shlomo HaMelech: "Many are the thoughts of men, but Hashem's council stands."[2] Shlomo HaMelech is teaching us that man has many ideas of what is important. However, he should know that the only thing that really stands and that really has

---

2   *Mishlei* 19:21.

importance and value is *atzas Hashem*—God's advice to us. Anything beyond *ratzon Hashem* is a man-made creation with the backing of the *yetzer hara*.

May we merit to constantly live and grow with this lesson. In doing so, we will benefit on so many levels. It will allow us to loosen up and not be so uptight, and with that will come a much more enjoyable life in this world as well.

Sefer Devarim

Devarim

ROOM SERVICE

יָדַע שׁוֹר קֹנֵהוּ וַחֲמוֹר אֵבוּס בְּעָלָיו
יִשְׂרָאֵל לֹא יָדַע עַמִּי לֹא הִתְבּוֹנָן.

*An ox knows his owner and a donkey his
master's trough; Yisrael does not know,
my people do not consider.*

Yeshayahu 1:3 (from the haftarah)

The *sefer Meaningful Messages* brings an explanation from the *sefer Toraso Yehegeh.*

Every day, without fail, the donkey goes to the same place that his owner places his food. He does not think for even one moment that perhaps his food may not be there. There is no doubt or hesitation in his mind. He has faith and relies on his owner. This was the admonition of the *navi* to B'nei Yisrael. If this is so for a donkey, how much more so should we place our faith in Hashem that He can, and He will, supply us with all of our needs!

The Gemara says, "It is as difficult for Hashem to give us sustenance as it was for Him to split the sea."[1] What can we understand this to mean? We know that there is nothing that is too difficult for Hashem.

---

1   *Pesachim* 118a.

What we are learning here is that while one may think that when it comes to *parnassah*, we have a big part in determining our fortune. Hashem is telling us that this is absolutely not the case. Just as by *k'rias Yam Suf* it was obvious to one and all that it was completely done by Hashem, so too, the way Hashem sends us our livelihood is exactly like the splitting of the sea; He does not need our help. Just as there are areas of our life that don't concern us because we assume that they are completely out of our realm of control, so too should we address our *parnassah*.

That's what it means when it says sustenance is as difficult as splitting the sea for Hashem. They are both the same level of difficulty for Him, i.e. not difficult at all! They are both the same. They are both not you, rather Him. Just like He split the sea without our help, so too He gives us all our needs without our help. They are both not hard for The One Above!

> It was the custom of Rabbi Zusha of Anipoli that after he finished davening Shacharis, he would open the window, and, lifting his eyes to the Heavens, would call out, "Master of the World, Zusha is very hungry and desires to eat something!" Every morning, his gabbai would wait until he heard Reb Zusha's appeal before bringing in Reb Zusha's morning meal of cake with a little schnapps.
>
> One morning, the gabbai thought to himself, "Why doesn't Reb Zusha ask me directly for his meal? In fact, who does he think he is fooling by calling out to God like that? He knows full well that I bring him his food every day." He decided that the next morning he would not bring Reb Zusha's meal when he called out. Finally, the truth would be clear.
>
> The next morning, Reb Zusha awoke early, as usual. He first went to the town mikvah to immerse himself in preparation for the day. The night had been a rainy one in Anipoli, and the streets of the town had already turned to rivers of mud. In order to get from one side of the street to another, one had to cross on narrow planks that were laid across the flowing mud. As Reb

Zusha was crossing in the direction of the mikvah, a man whom he didn't recognize, a guest in town, was coming toward Reb Zusha from the other side. When he saw Reb Zusha, gaunt, almost emaciated, dressed in rags, the stranger yelled out, "Tramp!" and with a laugh jumped up and down on the plank, causing Reb Zusha to fall into the mud.

Reb Zusha didn't say a word. He quietly and calmly picked himself out of the mud and continued on his way to the mikvah. When the man arrived back at the inn where he was staying, he couldn't help but brag to the innkeeper about his amusing prank. But the innkeeper didn't laugh so quickly. He asked the guest to describe the tramp whom he had catapulted into the mud. Upon hearing, he clapped his hands to his head and cried out in anguish, "Oy vey! Do you know what you did? That was not just some beggar. That was the Rebbe, Reb Zusha!"

Now it was the turn of the guest to cry out, "Oy vey," for Reb Zusha was known to all as a holy tzaddik. Trembling, the guest struck his chest and said, "Oy vey, what am I going to do now? What am I going to do!"

"Don't worry," exclaimed the innkeeper. "Listen to me. I know just what you should do: Every morning, after the tzaddik finishes davening, he opens the window and cries out, 'Master of the World, Zusha is very hungry and desires to eat something!' So, I'll prepare some cakes and some schnapps for you to take to him. When you hear him call out, go in immediately with this gift, offer it to him, and beg his forgiveness. I'm certain that he will forgive you wholeheartedly."

That morning, like every morning, after davening, Reb Zusha went into his room, opened the window, and called out, "Master of the World, Zusha is very hungry and desires to eat something!" The gabbai, upon hearing Reb Zusha, held his ground and waited to see what the outcome would be. "Let the Master of the World bring him his cake this morning," he laughed to himself. Suddenly, the door of the shul opened, and

a man holding a large plate of cakes and a bottle of schnapps
came. He went straight in, put the cakes on the table, and then
fell to the floor in grief, begging the tzaddik for his forgiveness
(which he was quickly granted).

Then the gabbai really understood that it really was the
Master of the World who brought Reb Zusha his breakfast
every morning.

Let us learn the lesson of the donkey. If he does not think twice about
his daily lunch, relying completely on his owner, we should do the same.

May we merit to live with clarity of mind to know who it all comes
from. It will make us more thankful to the Giver, and it will open us up
to give proper credit where credit is due.

GIVING CREDIT
WHERE CREDIT IS DUE

וָאֶקַּח אֶת רָאשֵׁי שִׁבְטֵיכֶם אֲנָשִׁים
חֲכָמִים וִידֻעִים וָאֶתֵּן אוֹתָם רָאשִׁים
עֲלֵיכֶם שָׂרֵי אֲלָפִים וְשָׂרֵי מֵאוֹת
וְשָׂרֵי חֲמִשִּׁים וְשָׂרֵי עֲשָׂרֹת וְשֹׁטְרִים
לְשִׁבְטֵיכֶם.

*So I took the heads of your tribes, men
wise and well-known, and I made them
heads over you, leaders over thousands,
leaders over hundreds, leaders over fifties,
and leaders over tens, and officers, over
your tribes.*

Devarim 1:15

Moshe Rabbeinu was recalling the travels and travails of B'nei
Yisrael in the *midbar*, and he mentions the appointments of
the different-ranked judges. This idea came from Yisro, the father-in-law
of Moshe. Why, then, is his name not mentioned at all?

169

The *Ramban* gives a few answers. His last answer is as follows: It could be that because they asked Hashem, and it was all done with His approval, therefore Yisro doesn't get credit for it.

This answer is difficult to understand. We know and believe that nothing happens without Hashem. Yet, we still are obligated to attribute thanks and credit to the messenger! Does this answer why Yisro wasn't mentioned?

If we go back to *Parashas Yisro*, there is an interesting *pasuk*. Yisro says to Moshe: "אִם אֶת הַדָּבָר הַזֶּה תַּעֲשֶׂה וְצִוְּךָ אֱלֹקִים וְיָכָלְתָּ עֲמֹד."[1] *Rashi* explains the *pasuk* to mean the following: "If Hashem commands you to do this (appointing different-level judges), then you will be able to stand. However, if Hashem holds back the plan, you will not be able to stand."

How could Yisro be so sure of himself? How can he say with confidence that you will only manage if Hashem allows you to follow through on **my plan**, and if He doesn't, there is no way you will be able to stand?

Perhaps we can understand *Rashi* differently. Yisro was actually taking no credit at all for his idea. Rather, he was telling Moshe Rabbeinu that he has an idea, but the idea itself will have no success unless it is the plan of Hashem. If Hashem commands you, the plan can stand. However, if Hashem says "no," then the plan cannot stand. He was actually declaring that the idea has nothing to do with him, because only a God-given thought will have the strength to succeed. Man has many thoughts, but they remain as thoughts unless they are also God's plan. Yisro was referring to the plan and not to Moshe. You, Moshe, will be OK; Hashem will take care of you. But the idea that I present—who knows? It depends on what Hashem wants. Because Yisro was able to acknowledge that it is all in the hands of Hashem, he was given a *parashah* in the Torah that was named for him.

We are told to give a tenth of our money to charity, and from it we will become wealthy. We would assume that the best way to become affluent is by saving and not spending. However, when we acknowledge that it is all Hashem's and we do what he tells us to do with it, it creates

---

1   *Shemos* 18:23.

more wealth. In Babylon, they had a quote: "If you want to preserve your money, then give it to charity." The more we can separate ourselves from our success, the more blessing we allow into our lives.

Reb Moshe Reichman supported many Jewish institutions. One of his grandchildren once needed a favor from a certain school, so his parent (Mr. Reichman's son) asked his father (Moshe Reichman himself) to call the school that he was supporting and request that they do such and such. Moshe Reichman responded, "I have the *zechus* of giving tzedakah to the school, but it is up to the school and their educators to make any important decisions. That has absolutely nothing to do with me." He was somebody who did not use his success as a way to get the school to listen to him. He understood, like Yisro, that he is merely using the gift that Hashem has given him to further Torah study.

May we merit having God-inspired ideas and the strength to implement them in a Godly way so that they bring the world closer to its purpose.

Va'eschanan

IN THE THICK OF THINGS

רְאֵה לִמַּדְתִּי אֶתְכֶם חֻקִּים וּמִשְׁפָּטִים
כַּאֲשֶׁר צִוַּנִי ה׳ אֱלֹקָי לַעֲשׂוֹת כֵּן
בְּקֶרֶב הָאָרֶץ.

Behold, I have taught you statutes
and ordinances, as Hashem, my God,
commanded me, to do so in the midst
of the land.

Devarim 4:5

When the Torah was given, there were those that were of the opinion that to achieve the highest level of holiness, they must distance themselves from all worldly matters. If they go into complete isolation and cut themselves off from society, then they will find success in their Torah learning. Therefore, the Torah says "in the midst of the land," for we must be among others. In this world, we are expected to keep Torah in the proper way. Hashem doesn't want us to reject something that doesn't seem to have any higher purpose. He wants us to take the world that we were born into and become holy through elevating this world.

On that note, "in the midst of the land" also teaches us the following: It is crucial that the conduct we have in shul, or with a Rav, or at a *shiur*

172

is carried over into the way we express ourselves at work. Holy speech and conduct shouldn't be reserved for what we consider to be spiritual endeavors. Just as we would guard our eyes by sitting on the other side of the *mechitzah* at shul, let's be mindful that *"b'kerev ha'aretz,"* as we venture out into the land such as work, we should aim for that as well. We don't leave God at the train station and pick Him up when we arrive back at home. He comes with us "in the midst of the land," and we have opportunities to seek Him out wherever we find ourselves.

When the Torah was about to be given to man, the angels began to protest.[1] Hashem told Moshe to respond to the angels after assuring him protection. Moshe proceeded to show the angels that the Torah is filled with laws that apply to humans and not angels. For example, honor your parents. "Do you have parents?" asked Moshe Rabbeinu. The Torah says don't steal. "Do you have jealousy and desire other people's objects?" asked Moshe Rabbeinu. Even though the angels eventually agreed, they also already knew all of Moshe's arguments. If so, what had been their initial claim? They based themselves on the verse: "Place Your splendor on the Heavens and not on the land."[2] That is what they had assumed made sense, but they quickly realized that the purpose of the Torah was *"b'kerev ha'aretz"*—not in the heavens but amongst the mortals.

I was once at a beautiful event. The shul where the event took place was a state-of-the-art building with a majestic *Aron Kodesh*. The catered food was sumptuous: omelet stations, waffles—you name it, it was there. There was just one problem. When the *baal ha'simchah* got up to speak, you could not hear a word that he said; the crowd was too busy talking that they spoke right over him and showed him no respect. The chandeliers and black-tie waiters suddenly lost their appeal, because the crowd didn't seem to understand. The purpose of it all was to enhance and elevate the *simchah*, which didn't seem apparent from their actions.

We were given a state-of-the-art world. Hashem doesn't expect us to climb a mountain and sit in solitude. He doesn't expect us to accept

---

1   See *Shabbos* 88b–89a.
2   *Tehillim* 8:2.

month-long fasts. He wants us to live with all of the beauty, enjoy it all, and remember that He is the *Baal ha'simchah*, and it's all here to enhance our relationship with Him.

May we merit to take this message with us in the midst of the land. May we find the joy in using the beauty He has given us to serve Him.

Eikev

OUR BATTLE CRY

וּשְׁמַרְתֶּם אֶת כָּל הַמִּצְוָה אֲשֶׁר אָנֹכִי
מְצַוְּךָ הַיּוֹם לְמַעַן תֶּחֶזְקוּ וּבָאתֶם
וִירִשְׁתֶּם אֶת הָאָרֶץ אֲשֶׁר אַתֶּם
עֹבְרִים שָׁמָּה לְרִשְׁתָּהּ.

And you shall guard all the mitzvah that
I command you this day, in order that you
may be strong and come and possess the
land to which you are crossing, to possess it.

Devarim 11:8

This *pasuk*, says the *Ohr Hachaim Hakadosh*, is coming to counter the opinion of so many disillusioned individuals. There are those who say that in order to properly wage war and conquer Eretz Yisrael, we must take a break from Torah study and focus all of our attention on a successful battle strategy. The Torah responds with this *pasuk*, saying that that is not the case. On the contrary, "You shall guard all the **mitzvah**," says the *pasuk*. It doesn't say "mitzvos" in the plural form, but rather mitzvah in the singular. Says the *Ohr Hachaim*, this "mitzvah" is a reference to the one mitzvah of being actively involved in the study of Torah. If you do that, says the *pasuk*, then you will be strong, and you will get the land.

175

The study of Torah will actually make you stronger. Popular belief dictates that only physical strength training can help us on the battlefield. The *pasuk* teaches us that all strength comes from Hashem, and He is telling us exactly how to conquer the enemy.

The same is true for our personal conquest of land. Hashem is telling us that we should allow Him to give us what He'd like to give us, because as we know, "Hashem wants to give the Jewish People so much good, therefore he gave us so many different mitzvos and parts of Torah."[1] Hashem looks for excuses to give good to His children. He loves us so much, and He is always looking to send us His blessings.

As we strive for success, it is very easy to lose sight and start cutting corners or miss out on our spiritual responsibilities. We think that the minyan or *chavrusa* will make us miss out on a new deal. It is the total opposite. Your davening and learning are the **key** to your success!

The *pasuk* says, "I am understanding, and to Me there is strength."[2] With Torah, with this book of knowledge and understanding, one can attain the ultimate strength. Hashem is the benefactor of all knowledge and all understanding. He grants us this gift when we show our inner strength. When we overcome, overpower, and remain true to His Torah, then Hashem says, "This is precious to Me."

There was a young man who was going for an interview for a new job. It was during *sefirah*, and as such he had an unkempt beard growing. He was not sure if he should shave or not; after all, it was for *parnassah*! He decided to shave. During the interview, the non-Jewish CEO asked him, "I see that you are a religious Jew. If so, why are you clean-shaven? I heard from some of my Jewish friends that you should not shave during these days." His answer did not impress the boss. He did not get the job, as the boss said, "If you are not faithful to your faith, how do I know that you will be faithful at work?" (Obviously, one should not take this as a halachic *p'sak* not to shave during *sefirah*. However, as this is a true story, we can take a lesson from it into the rest of our life.)

---

1   *Makkos* 3:16.

2   *Mishlei* 8:14.

May we merit the conquering of the little cities within ourselves, and this should eventually lead us to conquering the ultimate city, Yerushalayim.

DON'T SETTLE

פֶּן תֹּאכַל וְשָׂבָעְתָּ וּבָתִּים טֹבִים
תִּבְנֶה וְיָשָׁבְתָּ.

Maybe you will eat and be sated, and build
good houses and dwell therein.

Devarim 8:12

וְאָמַרְתָּ בִּלְבָבֶךָ כֹּחִי וְעֹצֶם יָדִי עָשָׂה
לִי אֶת הַחַיִל הַזֶּה.

And you will say to yourself, "My strength
and the might of my hand has accumulated
this wealth for me."

Devarim 8:17

The concern that man will attribute his success to his own doing is so prevalent, says the Saba of Kelm, that the *pasuk* doesn't say, "maybe you will say," but rather, "you will say." Back in *pasuk* 12, it says פֶּן—"maybe you will build big homes." That part is a maybe, as it is possible that you will not become wealthy and therefore not build a large home. However, if you do become wealthy, you will say...

How very powerful are these words. Is there any hope? Is there any way that we can navigate wealth and God?

Of course we can! In the same *pasuk* that tells us that we will build good homes, it ends off with the words, "and you will settle in it." If we choose to settle into our wealth, i.e., if we choose to feel completely at ease and totally comfortable with a luxurious life, with that being the end with no higher calling, then we will end up saying that it was all our own doing. However, if we make the conscious decision not to settle in—if we don't make the house, the car, the pool, or the vacations our **life mission**, then we will be able to live with a higher understanding.

> A Yid came to Rav Meir Yechiel of Ostrovitz complaining about *parnassah*. His father had bequeathed him a textile factory, and his father had always done well. But ever since he had taken over, he was only losing money. Sometimes an entire day would pass without even one customer! "Do you give *tzedakah?*" asked the Rebbe.
>
> "Certainly," the Yid responded."
>
> "Tell me," asked the Rebbe, "how do you occupy your time when there are no customers?"
>
> "To be honest," he answered, "I sit and wait and do nothing at all."
>
> "That is the issue. When your father ran the store, he did not waste a moment. Between each customer, he was either learning or saying Tehillim, therefore, the yetzer hara sent him many customers to interrupt his learning. You, however, the yetzer hara has no need to disturb with customers."

By both father and son, it was not the work that determined the success; it was the time that they didn't work that brought their livelihood. The first step is to acknowledge that it is not our work or our hands that bring the *parnassah*, and the second step is to know how to direct our energy—whether it is in between or even during work when we have a moment. Do we bring a *sefer* to the workplace, or do we leave that at home?

The *Meilitz Yosher* shares an amazing insight. We wash our hands in the morning to cleanse our body of the residue of impurity that leaves its mark on our hands. Why the hands and not any other limbs?

He explains that man ascribes his success in the material world to the prowess of his hands—*kochi v'otzem yadi*. There is no greater impurity than this sort of mindset.

If we look two *pesukim* further, it says: "If you forget your God and you follow other gods..." Gods can come in many forms, not just the brick-and-mortar image we have in our head. It is any power other than Hashem that we allow to dominate our mindset.

The *pasuk* says: "נָתוֹן תִּתֵּן לוֹ וְלֹא יֵרַע לְבָבְךָ בְּתִתְּךָ לוֹ כִּי בִּגְלַל הַדָּבָר הַזֶּה יְבָרֶכְךָ ה' אֱלֹקֶיךָ בְּכָל מַעֲשֶׂךָ וּבְכֹל מִשְׁלַח יָדֶךָ."[1] The Torah says to give tzedakah and help out the poor, and in return Hashem will help us and bless us.

We can take this a step further: "כִּי בִּגְלַל הַדָּבָר"—Hashem blessed you in order for you to give tzedakah! The money and blessings that you have are given to you so that you can help others and acknowledge that its purpose is for Torah.

May we merit to purify our hands and hearts with the knowledge that it is never our handiwork that brings us *hatzlachah*. Once we understand this, we won't settle into the homes of this world. We will live with the awareness that it is all to serve a higher goal.

---

1   *Devarim* 15:10.

Re'eh

WEAR YOUR HEART ON YOUR SLEEVE

וְלֹא־תֹאכַל הַנֶּפֶשׁ עִם הַבָּשָׂר.

And you shall not eat the soul with the flesh.
Devarim 12:23

The *Talelei Oros* quotes the Vilna Gaon, who explains this *pasuk* to mean the following: Anyone who invests the bulk of his time, energy, money, and talent into his material desires and possessions will have "eaten meat," so to speak, but he will also have "consumed his soul." By allowing his worldly desires to take so much out of him, he allows his soul to be sold in the process.

Our truest passions in life are very visible on us. If we invest our energies into the meat, it's easily seen. When we invest our energies into the soul, our demeanor and face will show that as well. The *pasuk* says that "the wisdom of man shines on his face."[1] When man is truly invested in his internal *avodah* and not his external *avodah*, his eyes display his inner passions as well.

---

1   *Koheles* 8:1.

181

Rav Leib Chasman earned his livelihood selling flour in a small shop. One day, after closing the shop, he went to the Talmud Torah of Kelm to learn a bit. Rav Simcha Zissel of Kelm saw him and mentioned that he had flour on his sleeve. Rav Leib Chasman returned home, sat himself down, and began to make a calculation of his different accounts. When he finished, he told his wife, "According to my figures, we have enough in stock to pay back all of our creditors. I am going to take care of that, close the store, and spend time learning in Volozhin." His wife was very surprised and asked him to explain. He told her, "If the flour I sell is sticking to my sleeves, that means I've invested too much into my business. The time has come for me to return to yeshiva."

This is an obviously high level of priority, yet the lesson is clear. We wear what we do. The Gemara says that Rav Yochanan referred to his clothing as *mechabdosai*—that which honors me.[2] Clothing themselves are not bringing intrinsic honor to a person. Yet, they imply what we truly think is important. For instance, if one dresses nicely for Shabbos, it shows that one honors the holy day. If one dress up for some events and not for others, it is indicative of a deeper value. Clothing can also symbolically represent one's external features, disposition, *middos*, and the way one carries oneself. How we act externally is an outgrowth of what we are focused on internally.

The *parashah* opens up with רְאֵה אָנֹכִי—this can be explained as saying the same as the "*Anochi*" of אָנֹכִי ה׳ אֱלֹקֶיךָ. When we look to find God in everybody and everything, then we will not get easily consumed by the meat, by the physical pursuits that have no real external gain. We won't allow trivial matters to eat us up, and we won't sell our soul in the process of making a *parnassah*.

May we merit an external Godly glow that emanates from something much greater than anything this material world can offer.

---

2   *Shabbos* 113a.

Shoftim

LOCATION, LOCATION, LOCATION

וְעָשִׂיתָ עַל פִּי הַדָּבָר אֲשֶׁר יַגִּידוּ לְךָ
מִן הַמָּקוֹם הַהוּא אֲשֶׁר יִבְחַר ה׳
וְשָׁמַרְתָּ לַעֲשׂוֹת כְּכֹל אֲשֶׁר יוֹרוּךָ.

And you shall do according to the word they
tell you, from the place Hashem will choose,
and you shall observe to do according to all
they instruct you.

Devarim 17:10

his verse is referring to the Jewish court system. There are
times when difficult issues arise, and the Torah tells us to go to
the court in the Beis Hamikdash.

The Netziv points out that the Torah is stressing the point of מִן
הַמָּקוֹם הַהוּא twice—once in verse 8 and again in verse 10. What is the
reason for that?

Look to the judges for answers. It is not because they are smarter
than the litigants, as perhaps they are not. Yet the reason we follow
their ruling explicitly is because the chosen "place" is very helpful to
dictate halachah in the truest form.

Although *chochmah* is an obvious prerequisite to being a judge, there is still something that supersedes even this called, "*siyata d'Shmaya*—help from Above. And in the place that Hashem has chosen, there is an abundance of Godly guidance.

On a similar note, when B'nei Yisrael would go to be *oleh la'regel*, there were no signs helping them with directions. However, when a person accidentally killed another and needs to go to a city of refuge, there were signs helping him find his way there. What is the difference between the two?

The obvious difference is that the person running to the city of refuge was frantically running for his life. Time was of the essence. Signs were needed so that he can quickly escape danger. However, those making their way up to the Beis Hamikdash during the *Shalosh Regalim* were in no imminent danger. Another difference is as follows: how embarrassing it would be to the person running to the city of refuge to have to ask people how to get there, as it would indicate that he had killed somebody. Not so for those who were being *oleh la'regel*. Finally, says the Chafetz Chaim, a person who kills accidentally still killed. We don't want people to be negatively influenced by him, so we limit the need for him to interact with others by placing signs that show him the way to the city of refuge. However, those on the way to the mitzvah of *aliyah la'regel* are encouraged to interact with others and possibly influence them to join along in the mitzvah of going up to the Beis Hamikdash.

In this last answer, we see the unbelievable importance placed on our surroundings. Whether it is the judges in the Beis Hamikdash, those walking to the Beis Hamikdash or, God forbid, those running away after having killed, where we are matters!

When we choose where to live, where to work, or where to travel, there is tremendous consideration that should be put into the location. Where will I be positively affected by my surroundings? Which location will strengthen my family so that we can properly grow closer to Hashem?

May we merit to live like the tefillah of David HaMelech, "שִׁבְתִּי בְּבֵית ה' כָּל יְמֵי חַיַּי לַחֲזוֹת בְּנֹעַם ה' וּלְבַקֵּר בְּהֵיכָלוֹ"—I will sit in the house of Hashem, all the days of my life, and see the pleasantness of Hashem, and visit His sanctuary."[1] Although we may not be in the *beis midrash* all day, our yearning is to return there as soon as we can.

---

1   *Tehillim* 27:4.

NO COWARDICE
IN THE ARMY OF HASHEM

מִי הָאִישׁ אֲשֶׁר בָּנָה בַיִת חָדָשׁ
וְלֹא חֲנָכוֹ...וּמִי הָאִישׁ אֲשֶׁר נָטַע
כֶּרֶם...וּמִי הָאִישׁ אֲשֶׁר אֵרַשׂ אִשָּׁה
וְלֹא לְקָחָהּ.

What man is there who has built a new
house and has not [yet] inaugurated
it?...And what man is there who has
planted a vineyard, and has not [yet]
redeemed it?...And what man is there who
has betrothed a woman and has not [yet]
taken her?

Devarim 20:5–7

These were specific people and their specific circumstances that were exempt from fighting battles when B'nei Yisrael went out to war. Why were they not required to fight? The Torah says because somebody else "may take their home, their vineyard, or their wife." A person would not be able to concentrate on war when he was concerned about these matters. Others explain that he will be depressed, and the sad thoughts will make him unable to fight. Therefore, the Torah tells him to go home.

It seems as though this person is lacking proper *emunah*. If he truly believes that Hashem is taking care of his home, his vineyard, and his wife, then why is he unable to clear his mind and fight properly? Why does the Torah allow such a person to return home?

The empowering lesson here is that Hashem, who created the human mind and heart, understands what is within our ability and what is not. He exempts us from the battle during certain times when He knows that it is beyond what is expected of us. This gives us tremendous strength as we work on all of the 613 commandments. If He commanded us to do them, that means that Hashem has complete belief that we can do them; we can succeed. If we couldn't, He would exempt us as He did in this *parashah*.

The Torah was discussing exemptions in relation to the battles and wars that we were fighting. We all fight our own inner battles—how we deal with others, how we control our anger, and so on. Hashem is telling us that we will not win every battle, and we are sometimes exempt from battles during particular times. What this means for us is that if we are obligated in something, we must give it our all and try our best, because we are capable. "If we build a house or plant a vineyard" are terms that show preoccupation with *parnassah*. "If we just got engaged" is a term of family responsibility. All of these different worldly matters can preoccupy our mind. Sometimes there are a thousand thoughts during a short *Shemoneh Esreh*. Hashem is telling us not to worry, and we don't need to tire ourselves out from the fight. All that's asked of us is that we do what we can when we are able.

The *parashah* ends off by saying, "Those who are afraid should re-turn home." The Gemara explains this to mean that one may be afraid because of sins that he may have committed. This man is told, "You need to return and go home."[1] This is the gift of *teshuvah* that Hashem has so lovingly given us. Do not fall apart and think that you are not

---

1   *Sotah 44a.*

capable; don't assume that you will never be able to fight battles. You can and you will, and you can always return home.

The *tzaddikim* tell us that the worst sin is not a sin. Instead, it is *atzvus*—depression. It is one of the strongest tools of the *yetzer hara*. He uses it to make us feel unworthy and incapable. We need to remind ourselves that if Hashem commanded us, He deems us capable and worthy.

May we merit the strength to fight our battles and the knowledge to know when it is time to go home. May we soon see the day that the Navi says, "וְלֹא יִלְמְדוּ עוֹד מִלְחָמָה—There will be no more wars to be waged,"[2] with the coming of Mashiach.

---

2 *Yeshayahu* 2:4.

Ki Seitzei

DEEP POCKETS

הָשֵׁב תְּשִׁיבֵם לְאָחִיךָ.

You shall return them to your brother.

Devarim 22:1

In this week's *parashah*, we are taught about the mitzvah of hashavas *aveidah*—returning a lost item. With regard to money, the halachah normally dictates that the finder may keep it, being that there is no *siman*—no specific sign that would prevent the owner from relinquishing hope of it being returned to him. We can assume that by the time the finder chanced upon it, the owner has already given up hope of finding it. This is known as *yei'ush*, which means that the owner knows he's lost it and has given up hope of finding it.

How can we be so sure that the owner is aware of his loss? Maybe he has not yet realized that he lost it, and if this were to be the case, the finder would not be able to keep it as the owner still retains ownership over it.

The Gemara says that there is an accepted assumption when it comes to money that "אָדָם עָשׂוּי לְמַשְׁמֵשׁ בְּכִיסוֹ בְּכָל שָׁעָה וְשָׁעָה—A person constantly checks his pockets to feel for his money."[1] This leads us to understand

---

1   *Bava Metzia* 21b.

that if the money has fallen out, we can safely assume that the owner is aware of the fact. The Gemara applies this lesson to all people. It is the nature of people to know if they are carrying money in their pockets.

Can we say the same about ourselves when it comes to our spiritual wealth and our spiritual pockets? Are there certain valuables and treasures that we constantly check on? Are we aware of the time so that we know if we need to be davening? Are we early to show up so that we don't even miss a minute of *tefillah*? Do we know the *z'manei tefillah* for Shabbos and Yom Tov, or do we allow ourselves to rely on other people? Which pockets are we constantly checking?

Later in the *parashah*, it says, "When you come into your friend's vineyard and eat grapes to sate your soul, you should not put them in your vessel." The *Parashah Anthology* quotes the *Mikdash Mordechai*, which says that the *pasuk* is telling us that we should take enough to satiate our soul. When you eat until satiation, you do not worry about the future; you make sure that you have what you need for now. A person who lives this way does not need to accumulate massive stockpiles of provisions for a later date; he is satisfied. The believer sees little need to fill and overfill his material pockets. True, he must take care of himself and his family, but only to a certain extent.

During a food shortage in Eretz Yisrael, the Brisker Rav's daughter complained to her father that the prices keep on rising. How are we going to be able to buy food? The Brisker Rav responded, "The Gemara says that 'כָּל מְזוֹנוֹתָיו שֶׁל אָדָם קְצוּבִים לוֹ מֵרֹאשׁ הַשָּׁנָה'—One's sustenance is determined on Rosh Hashanah.[2] It does not say how much money one will make, rather מְזוֹנוֹת—food, regardless of the price. Hashem has already decided how much we will have. There is no need to worry!"

May we merit pockets that are full with our material needs and overflow with our spiritual wealth.

---

2   *Beitzah* 16a.

Ki Savo

THE FRUITS OF OUR LABOR

וְשָׂמַחְתָּ בְכָל הַטּוֹב אֲשֶׁר נָתַן לְךָ.

Then, you shall rejoice with all the goodness
that Hashem, your God, has given you.
Devarim 26:11

This is referring to the mitzvah of *bikkurim*, which takes place after the crops start to ripen. Amidst tremendous celebration, the farmer takes his first fruits and brings them to Yerushalayim. This is considered the happiest time for the farmers, as their entire year's work is finally "bearing fruit." Now is when they get to see the profit. After all of their hard work, they can finally enjoy the fruits of their labor.

Why then does the Torah have to tell the farmer "you shall rejoice"? Wouldn't we assume that he is naturally rejoicing and full of happiness? After all, today is the day that he will finally get his paycheck and receive all that he's been waiting for!

Rabbi Yissachar Frand tells us that the Torah needs to obligate him to be happy because it is natural human tendency to want more and be dissatisfied the moment we receive something.

The *pasuk* is not only telling us to be happy but it is also giving us the key to find that happiness. It says, "Rejoice...with all the goodness that **Hashem has given you**," remembering that what we have is a gift.

Knowing that it is not coming to us and understanding that it is not a result of what we deserve will facilitate inner happiness. Who doesn't love receiving a gift? Furthermore, if this is what was given to us, it is exactly what we are supposed to have. Lastly, the *pasuk* ends off, "You and the Levi," meaning: "Remember why I gave you the success. It is to help the Levi who works in the Beis Hamikdash; it is in order to give charity. You are a deliveryman, bringing My goods to My children."

My friend told me the following story of someone who was once approached to help out with a certain tzedakah. The person immediately jumped at the opportunity and gave an open check! It turned out that the money was never needed, and it all worked out. The one who jumped at the mitzvah gets reward! He did his *chelek*. Ultimately, everything is up to Hashem who doesn't need our help. Rather, He gives us the chance to be a holy messenger. All the money is His; we have the chance to deliver it. This person did exactly that!

When the person would bring his *bikkurim*, the Kohen would place his hands under the person's hands, and together they would wave it. I was thinking that possibly this is to be a constant reminder that it is not from our hands and not just from our hard work. The Torah purposely says let the Kohen's hands also hold it so that you shouldn't think it is from your hands!

The farmer had to tie a piece of reed grass around his first fruits to set them aside for *bikkurim*. This grass was called גמי, which stands for "גְּדֹלִים מַעֲשֵׂי ה׳—God's creations are great."[1]

May we merit experiencing tremendous joy that comes from the knowledge that all that we are given is a gift, and that all of His creations are great.

---

1   *Tehillim* 111:2.

Nitzavim

HOME SWEET HOME

וְשָׁב ה׳ אֱלֹקֶיךָ אֶת שְׁבוּתְךָ וְרִחֲמֶךָ
וְשָׁב וְקִבֶּצְךָ מִכָּל הָעַמִּים אֲשֶׁר
הֱפִיצְךָ ה׳ אֱלֹקֶיךָ שָׁמָּה.

Then, Hashem, your God, will return back
your exiles, and He will have mercy upon
you. He will once again return you from all
the nations, where Hashem, your God, had
dispersed you.

Devarim 30:3

Why does the *pasuk* say "He will return" twice? The second
half of the verse seems like a repetition of the first.

The *Meshech Chochmah* says that Hashem will take two types of Jews
out of captivity. There are those who are constantly yearning for *geulah*.
They have a deep desire to get to Eretz Yisrael, and they want to escape
galus as a prisoner who runs from captivity. Hashem will redeem them
first. When the *pasuk* says, "He will have mercy on you," it is a reference
to these Jews.

Then there are those who have become very comfortable in *galus*.
They do not have daily yearnings for *geulah* and Eretz Yisrael. Those,
too, Hashem will redeem, as the *pasuk* says, "He will gather." Yet, they

will need to be taken. Only after the first group returns will they have the opportunity to go.

When B'nei Yisrael came down to Egypt, the tribes said to Pharaoh, "We have come to sojourn in the land." They referred to themselves as "strangers." The *mefarshim* explain that because they realized it was not their land, they eventually merited leaving Mitzrayim.

While we are always thankful to our host lands that allow us temporary dwelling, the Torah is teaching us to remember that we are merely guests.

On a personal level, do we consider the Beis Hashem "our place," or do we feel more at home when we're behind our desk or when we're walking through the streets of Manhattan? The Gemara says that all *batei midrashos* will become part of Eretz Yisrael in the future. This means that even in *galus*, there are places that are semi-removed from the foreign lands, acting as an embassy for *kedushah*. Within them, we can bask in the holiness of the *Shechinah*. We have the ability and the responsibility to make our homes *batei midrashos*. What we discuss at our table and what we invest our passion into will determine whether our homes will have a spirit of *galus*, *chas v'shalom*, or a spirit of *geulah*.

The story is told of a certain *tzaddik* who always yearned for Mashiach. One Erev Shabbos, as they waited for his son-in-law to come, the hour was getting late, and he still had not arrived. The *tzaddik* was preparing for Shabbos when he heard people yelling, "He's here!" The *tzaddik* dropped what he was doing and came running. When he saw his son-in-law, he fainted. After they revived him, he explained: "True, I am happy that my son-in-law arrived. However, when they yelled that 'He's here,' I thought they were referring to Mashiach. I was so excited that after all these years I was going to see Mashiach. And then I saw that it was not the case. That is why I fainted."

May we merit that our external yearnings should match the yearnings of our soul, the yearning for the ultimate *geulah*. May we soon see the day that we all return, and may we belong to the group that is immediately brought to Eretz Yisrael "with God's mercy."

Vayelech

NO NEED TO WORRY

הַקְהֵל אֶת הָעָם הָאֲנָשִׁים
וְהַנָּשִׁים וְהַטָּף.

Assemble the people: the men, the women,
and the children.

Devarim 31:12

Hakhel takes place when three big events collide: First, it is at the end of Sukkos. Second, it is at the end of a *shemittah* year. And third, it is at the time when B'nei Yisrael are *oleh la'regel*.

These three times, says Rabbi Avraham Gurwitz, Rosh Yeshiva of Gateshead Yeshiva, all have a common theme—the mitzvah of *bitachon*. On Sukkos, we sit in "the tent of faith." The sukkah reminds us Who sheltered us in the desert and Who continues to shelter us. During *shemittah*, we put our financial future in the hands of Hashem, and for *aliyah la'regel*, we leave our homes unattended and trust that Hashem will watch all our belongings when we travel to the Beis Hamikdach.

Why do these three events connect to the mitzvah of *hakhel*?

The Torah says that the purpose of the mitzvah of *hakhel* was "to hear and learn to have fear of Hashem, and to be careful to perform all of the words of His Torah." What is the most effective way to teach someone to keep all the mitzvos? What is the common denominator of them all?

195

אָנֹכִי ה' אֱלֹקֶיךָ—the belief in Hashem and in all that He commanded. As the saying goes, "With belief, there are no questions. Without belief, there are no answers."

> *The Baal Shem Tov once told his chassidim, "I want you to travel to a certain inn so that you can learn firsthand what it means to truly believe in Hashem." They happily traveled, and when they arrived, the innkeeper graciously opened his doors to them. After eating a warm meal, they sat down to learn and were joined by the innkeeper. A short while later, there was a knock on the door, and standing there was an officer. He then turned around and left. A few hours later, the same thing happened again: the officer knocked, and then he left. Eventually, the chassidim inquired of the innkeeper as to the meaning of all of this. He told them that he owed the poritz a significant amount of money, and he only had a few hours left to pay before he would be harshly punished.*
>
> *"So why didn't you pay the officer?" the chassidim asked.*
>
> *The innkeeper replied, "I don't have the money."*
>
> *The chassidim said, "But you don't seem concerned at all."*
>
> *He answered, "Hashem will take care of it; there is nothing for me to worry about."*
>
> *He continued learning with them until the time came for him to pay. He put on his coat and walked out of the inn. The chassidim decided to follow closely behind him. After a short time, a carriage pulled up alongside the innkeeper. Somebody spoke with him and then handed him an envelope. He continued on his way to the poritz, paid him, and then returned back. He explained to the amazed chassidim that somebody wanted to buy a lot of beer for the upcoming year, and he had just paid him in advance—the entire sum was in that envelope. And just as he had believed all along, Hashem had provided.*

As these three special events came together, B'nei Yisrael were able to strengthen their *bitachon* in Hashem and were left with a strong result—that they are capable of keeping the entire Torah.

May we merit to continuously strengthen our belief in Hashem. May we always feel that both ourselves and our finances are protected, and may we soon come to see the ultimate הַקְהֵל—with all of Klal Yisrael coming together in the Beis Hamikdash, with the coming of Mashiach.

Haazinu

HEAVEN ON EARTH

הַאֲזִינוּ הַשָּׁמַיִם וַאֲדַבֵּרָה
וְתִשְׁמַע הָאָרֶץ אִמְרֵי פִי.

*Listen, O heavens, and I will speak! And let
the earth hear the words of my mouth!*

Devarim 32:1

There are times when we feel that we are on a spiritual high, so to speak. For some, it's after a fabulous *shiur* or a strong davening, and for many, it is after they have gone through the *Yamim Nora'im*. This *pasuk* is telling us that it is not enough to experience these feelings, but we must channel them down to earth and integrate all of these spiritual emotions in our daily, very busy, and often mundane, lives. It is not enough that our spirituality is *"l'sheim Shamayim"*—our *gashmiyus* lives must also be filled with Hashem.

Rabbi Yoni Levin, of Congregation Aish Kodesh, once said that this is the lesson of this week's *haftarah*. "קְחוּ עִמָּכֶם דְּבָרִים וְשׁוּבוּ אֶל ה׳—Take these words with you and return to Hashem."[1] Take the elevated feelings of *hisorerus* and *teshuvah* into your days and weeks ahead. Bring it to your family, your work, and your daily interactions.

---

1   *Hoshea* 14:3.

Once, after a beautiful and uplifting *Yamim Nora'im*, days filled with such pure *kedushah*, I asked Rabbi Moshe Weinberger, my Rav, "How do I go to work now?" He responded, "Take the Belt Parkway!" He was telling me that we don't run away from our daily obligations after experiencing a spiritual climax; we bring it along with us.

This is what Hashem was telling Noach when He said, "צֵא מִן הַתֵּבָה—Leave the ark." The *teivah* is a reference to a safe haven, not just in the physical sense, but a spiritual one as well. The land was filled with impurity, and it was there that Hashem kept Noach safe. Yet, when the time was right, Hashem instructed Noach to go out from the *teivah*—go out into the world, and it is there that you will fulfill your mission.

The *chassidim* say that מַשִּׁיב הָרוּחַ וּמוֹרִיד הַגֶּשֶׁם—let the *ruchniyus* "leave" and bring down the *gashmiyus*! Let the true *avodah* begin.

One of the most beautiful days of the year is Erev Yom Kippur. It is charged with anticipation and holiness. Meaningful phone calls take place, everyone is giving "*G'mar Chasimah Tovah*" wishes, and even the grocery store feels different. Nobody is annoyed at the guy who is paying with exact change; people offer to allow others to go ahead of them. You can literally feel that Yom Kippur is in the air. That is Heaven and Earth coming together.

"הַאֲזִינוּ הַשָּׁמַיִם...וְתִשְׁמַע הָאָרֶץ"—May we merit experiencing Heaven on Earth by taking all the meaningful moments that we experience and living with them every moment.

V'zos Haberachah

"A" FOR EFFORT

וְלִזְבוּלֻן אָמַר שְׂמַח זְבוּלֻן בְּצֵאתֶךָ
וְיִשָּׂשכָר בְּאֹהָלֶיךָ.

*And to Zevulun he said: "Rejoice, Zevulun,
in your departure, and Yissachar,
in your tents."*

Devarim 33:18

Rav Bezalel Rudinsky of Monsey, New York, asks the following:
We know that Zevulun was the one who went out to work in
order to support Yissachar. Isn't the main joy of work when we return
home at the end of a long day with our paycheck? Why does the Torah
tell Zevulun to rejoice when he goes out? It is hard. It can get dirty.
There are challenges, and sometimes we feel like we are wasting so
much time. The joy is usually felt later on.

However, based on the theme of this *sefer*, this *pasuk* can be easily
understood. When we work to serve Hashem, wherever we find ourselves, be it in shul or at the office, it is all *avodas Hashem*. There is
great joy that comes from the total awareness of fulfilling my mission,
whatever it may be. When I leave each morning, I can skip to work,
knowing that the day is open with limitless potential to serve Hashem.
Just like the reward for Torah is for the effort, not the product, so too

by work. The effort itself, regardless of the outcome, which many times falls through, gives us reward. What a gratifying lesson!

Tosafos asks: The Gemara says that the first question we will be asked after 120 is "נָשָׂאתָ וְנָתַתָּ בָּאֱמוּנָה—Did you deal honestly in business?"[1] However, a different Gemara (*Kiddushin* 40b) quotes Rav Hamnuna as saying that first a person will be judged by "קָבַעְתָּ עִתִּים לַתּוֹרָה—Did you make permanent times for Torah?"[2] This seems to be a contradiction.

The *mefarshim* answer that when one works honestly, and he follows Torah guidelines in how he conducts his business, and he sets aside time to learn, that is a fulfillment of the dictate of קָבַעְתָּ עִתִּים—he made his Torah permanent. His work has become *avodas Hashem*, because everything else was secondary to his primary goal of being an *eved Hashem*.

The Baal Shem Tov says that one who works in this fashion is being עוֹסֵק בַּתּוֹרָה—involved in Torah, for not only is he learning it, but he is practicing it as well.

The *Meor Einayim* takes this a step further. Through our *emunah* that Hashem fills every part of this world, from the holiest to the most mundane, we reveal the sparks of holiness that can be found in every time and place.

Both questions are really one and the same.

נָשָׂאתָ—Did you lift the item, the moment; וְנָתַתָּ —and place it in its source, in its true place? How is this done? בָּאֱמוּנָה—If you truly believe that it is all from Hashem. Living this way is a true fulfillment of קָבַעְתָּ עִתִּים לַתּוֹרָה—you have declared that all time, everywhere, and everything is truly Torah!

As we finish the *Chamishah Chumshei Torah*, we celebrate Simchas Torah. On this day of rejoicing, we take the Torah out and dance with it. We don't open the Torah (for a majority of the time). We hold it, hug it, and kiss it.

There are times that it can appear as though the Torah is closed, but it is really wide open.

---

1   *Shabbos* 31a.
2   *Tosafos, Kiddushin* 40b.

May we merit living lives with the joy that comes with the knowledge that every moment is so valuable, precious, and holy. May we feel the wealth and richness that comes from living a Torah life. And may we always feel, whether in shul or at work, that we are embracing the Torah and dancing with it with every step we take.

ABOUT THE AUTHOR

Jeff Weinberg grew up in Canarsie in Brooklyn, NY, and graduated Yeshiva University. He is the co-founding partner of Meridian Capital Group, a leading mortgage company, and is a board member of SoftWorks AI, a start-up software company. He is a long-time member of Congregation Aish Kodesh in Woodmere, New York, and has served as a board member and in various other roles in Chabad of the Five Towns, Yeshiva of South Shore, and NCSY. Jeff resides with his family in Woodmere, New York.

MOSAICA PRESS
BOOK PUBLISHERS

Elegant, Meaningful & Bold

info@MosaicaPress.com
www.MosaicaPress.com

The Mosaica Press team of
acclaimed editors and designers
is attracting some of the most
compelling thinkers and teachers
in the Jewish community today.
Our books are available around
the world.

HARAV YAACOV HABER
RABBI DORON KORNBLUTH